Contents

WWF is an international environmental organisation with national groups around the world. Launched in 1961, WWF has supported over 5,000 projects in 130 countries, and has invested over £230 million in conservation and education over the last 10 years.

WWF aims to conserve nature and ecological processes for the benefit of all life on Earth. By stopping, and eventually reversing the degredation of our natural environment, we strive for a future in which people and nature can live in balance. This mission can only be acheived if people recognise and accept the need for sustainable, just and careful use of natural resources. Education has a key role to play in the process.

WWF-UK is therefore committed to a broadly based environmental education programme. As part of this programme, it has initiated a wide range of curriculum development and community projects resulting in over 200 resources for home and school; publications designed to give people the skills and knowledge they need in order to make informed personal judgements about environmental issues. A Grant Award Scheme has also been set up to help schools formulate and practise whole school environmental policies.

"Reaching Out", WWF's INSET programme for both Primary and Secondary teachers and teacher trainers, is now available on a regional basis across the UK. We also have a number of innovative electronic data delivery projects which give schools, colleges and individuals access to WWF's expertise, data, reports and fact sheets.

In addition to courses and resources, WWF runs a free Teacher Representative Scheme for all schools. Registered schools receive WWF's termly teachers newsletter, *Lifelines*, details of new resources, plus a discount on all education materials.

If you would like further details about WWF's education programme, please write to: WWF-UK, Education & Awareness, Panda House, Weyside Park, Godalming, Surrey GU7 1XR. Telephone: 01483 426444. Fax: 01483 426409. Web site address: http://www.wwf-uk.org

CLARE MARLOW taught in primary schools for 23 years, specialising in English. For part of this time she was a member of a special needs advisory team for literacy in mid-Hampshire. She then moved into lecturing, and is currently working at La Sainte Union College in Southampton where she teaches BEd and PGCE students. Her first book was a general introduction to primary education and was published at the beginning of 1994.

JILL BRAND has a background of primary school teaching, educational television and educational publishing. She worked for 12 years as a staff member of the Inner London Education Authority Learning Resources Branch, where she learned a great deal from the wonderful classroom teachers who were seconded for particular projects. In recent years she has specialised in writing and editing material concerned with Environmental and Development Education, being firmly convinced that a sustainable future depends on the coming generations not repeating the mistakes of the present and past.

INTRODUCTION

Environmental Education – not another subject!

How much do you think about environmental issues? Are you worried about the state of the planet? Do you consider yourself well informed on such subjects as global warming, biodiversity, sustainable development? How relevant are they to children? What does the term 'Environmental Education' really mean? Is it part of the National Curriculum? How do we teach it? This book has been written to help you find some answers to these and similar questions. At various points throughout the book there are boxes headed 'Over to you' which give you a chance to evaluate your own position and your response to what you have read.

Environmental Education is not yet one more subject to be added to the compulsory ten in the National Curriculum for England and Wales. It is one of the five 'cross-curricular themes' which were originally set out as part of every pupil's entitlement to a broad and balanced curriculum. The other four are: Economic and Industrial Understanding, Health Education, Careers Education and Guidance, and Education for Citizenship (England), or Community Understanding (Wales). These all have links with Environmental Education and have the following characteristics:

> "Never has there been a greater need for young people to be aware of the necessity to look after the environment. They are its custodians, and will be responsible for the world in which, in turn, their children will grow up.
>
> It is essential that all those with influence over the environment work together towards its conservation and improvement. This means that schools must assume their responsibility for environmental education."
>
> CURRICULUM GUIDANCE 7: ENVIRONMENTAL EDUCATION

"...the ability to foster discussion of questions of values and beliefs; they add to knowledge and understanding and they rely on practical activities, decision making, and the inter-relationship of the individual and the community."

CURRICULUM GUIDANCE 3: THE WHOLE CURRICULUM

Much of the knowledge which children need to acquire about environmental issues is already covered in the National Curriculum subjects, particularly Science and Geography. But, as the quotation above clearly indicates, Environmental Education is about more than knowledge. Part 4 discusses more fully a variety of definitions and aims of Environmental Education which have been put forward over the last few years. The quotations there will show you that there is a wide range of views on what Environmental Education should be doing, and you should be aware that this book has its own particular orientation.

WILL ENVIRONMENTAL EDUCATION HELP ME?

Far from being one more subject to be squeezed into a crowded timetable, Environmental Education can actually be of great help to a school or a teacher in overall planning. Much school topic work is organised around environmental themes: the neighbourhood, Planet Earth, seas and oceans, energy... Teachers have seen this as a good way of integrating the individual subjects of the National Curriculum into a coherent pattern. If you think about that brief list above, you will easily see how the knowledge, skills and concepts of Geography, Science, History and Technology could fit into the topics. There could also be plenty of opportunities for work in English, Maths, Music, RE and Art. Perhaps you will also see ways of integrating Dance and PE.

CHILDREN AND THE ENVIRONMENT

Children seem naturally drawn to a sympathetic concern for our planet and all living things upon it. Is it romantic to think that this is because they still have an innocent affinity with the natural world, and instinctively feel at one with other living things? Cynics might say that the children's idealism is only possible because they cannot grasp the political and economic overtones which are the reality of modern life. One of the aims of Environmental Education is to teach children about these realities while building on their idealism.

> "We have to share the planet so don't be selfish. We want food to be shared so that everyone has enough. We want clean water and a home for all people. We are worried about pollution, and war and children starving, while others don't appreciate the food they get. We are afraid that the world will soon belong only to the rich."
>
> *FROM THE GLOBAL CHILDREN'S HEARING, HELD IN RIO DE JANEIRO AT THE SAME TIME AS THE EARTH SUMMIT, JUNE 1992*

Teachers should remember that schooling forms only part of children's education. We have only to think of the long-standing Blue Peter appeals. In many cases these annual efforts have been made in areas of recycling or conservation, and children have been the main motivating force behind adult support. Other children's programmes regularly draw attention to the plight of indigenous people, or threatened animal species.

Children are enthusiastic about what they can observe, hear, smell, experience and enjoy. All children, and young children in particular, are constantly trying to make sense of new experiences in the light of what they already know. If their learning can be linked to this exploration, then their curiosity will be engaged. Environmental Education is an obvious place to find effective experiential learning.

> *"The challenge for both teachers and pupils is to look again at the ordinary, everyday and perhaps banal features of our lives in a familiar environment, and invest them with a new meaning and significance which has wider relevance for our lives."*
>
> *A COMMON PURPOSE*

Although knowledge is important, children's learning will only really develop if they understand. Understanding means assimilating concepts thoroughly enough to be able to use them for original thinking. Children do this best when their emotions are engaged as well as their intellect. Our education system has the strange notion that once children have stopped being 'infants', there is less and less room for emotion. The citizens of tomorrow will need to find solutions to the problems of the planet with their hearts as well as their heads. If we, as teachers, fail to help them, then the children we teach will be entitled to speak as this excerpt from a poem speaks for them:

> *"You helped me extend my hands with incredible machines,*
> *my eyes with telescopes and microscopes,*
> *my ears with telephones, radar and sonar,*
> *my brain with computers, but you did not help me extend*
> *my heart, love, concern*
> *to the entire human family.*
> *You, teacher, gave me half a loaf."* JON RYE KINGHORN

ADULTS AND THE ENVIRONMENT

If children have taken the lead in some of the simpler areas of environmental concern, what have adults been doing? The last 20 years has been a time of changing attitudes. Governments have made their own responses, as Part 3 will describe, but what of individuals? As a general rule, the questions that have bothered individuals seem to have moved from the simple to the more far-reaching. Here are some examples:

Simple question: *"Does this spray-can contain CFCs?"*
More far-reaching question: *"Do I need to use a spray-can for this job?"*

Simple question: *"Will using disposable nappies use more or less energy than terry-towelling ones?"*
More far-reaching question: *"What happens to 'disposable' sanitary products in sewage systems or land-fill sites?"*

Simple question: *"How much pollution does a catalytic converter on my car prevent?"*
More far-reaching question: *"Can we go on building more and more large roads for more and more traffic?"*

Simple question: *"Is it safer to bury nuclear waste underground or to dump it at sea?"*
More far-reaching question: *"Can we go on using nuclear power which leaves such a deadly legacy for generations to come, and for which we have no technological answer?"*

Simple question: *"If I give money to help set up a wildlife conservation area in Africa, what will happen to the local people?"*
More far-reaching question: *"What are the trading systems between that country and richer countries of the North which put pressure on the local people to cut down the trees?"*

Simple question: *"Where is the nearest recycling centre?"*
More far reaching question: *"How have I managed to acquire so much stuff I now need to get rid of?"*

You may recognise your own thought processes in the questions above.

REFERENCES

CURRICULUM GUIDANCE 3:
THE WHOLE CURRICULUM
NCC, 1990

CURRICULUM GUIDANCE 7:
ENVIRONMENTAL EDUCATION *NCC, 1990*

Poem by Jon Rye Kinghorn from **EARTHRIGHTS:**
EDUCATION AS IF THE PLANET REALLY
MATTERED, *WWF-UK/Kogan Page, 1987*

A COMMON PURPOSE, *WWF-UK, 1988*

ENVIRONMENTAL EDUCATION AND YOUR TRAINING

In primary teacher training, the 1990s have been characterised by radical and continuous change and development. These changes affect the opportunities which you have to teach Environmental Education, because they provide the framework within which all involved in initial teacher training work.

The aims of this chapter are:
- to positively affirm how it is possible for you to use the new national framework for teacher training to enhance opportunities for teaching Environmental Education
- to identify where support for your professional development in Environmental Education might come from within this new framework.

A New National Framework for Teacher Training

Let us first take a look at what is meant by this idea of a new national framework for teacher training. In broad terms the changes that have come about in the way initial teacher training is organised are characterised by increased Government control. This whole process formally began in January 1992 when the then Education Secretary, Kenneth Clarke, made public his plans for an overhaul of teacher training. He made it quite clear that his intention was to give schools a more important role in training:

"the way to break the rules of dogma about classroom organisation and teaching methods was to give the teaching role in training to schools".

CLARKE, 1992

From this beginning flowed a number of policy documents which have led to Clarke's vision being realised. Particularly important were DfEE Circulars 9/92 and 14/93 which lay down the competencies which all newly qualified teachers are expected to achieve. It is these competencies which increasingly underpin all courses of teacher training. Essentially they specify the expectations about the level of competence you can be expected to achieve when you enter the profession. The reforms also placed increased emphasis on the role of schools in training and encouraged the development of SCITTs where training is almost entirely school based. At the same time as these reforms were occurring, an inspection system was created which made links between the 'new order' in teacher training and the allocation of funds to be provided. In other words, if institutions did not put into place the reforms, they would be penalised. Additionally the establishment of the Teacher Training

Agency (TTA) in 1994 was a major step in establishing greater control of teacher training, and in 1997 the new national curriculum for teacher training written by the TTA will ensure consistency between different providers. The experience of teacher training which you have should, in short, be comparable with other trainees in other institutions!

Why is it that these changes have been brought in? Well there are many different views on this but most importantly increased Government control is seen as having an indirect influence on the quality of teaching and learning in schools. It is about establishing new standards of excellence in teacher training so that there will be a knock-on effect in schools as new teachers come on stream. The view about it being necessary to reform provision stems in part from a right-wing perspective that teacher training peddles dangerous and possibly even subversive approaches. As Boyson (1996) writes: *"There is still a suspicion that teacher training institutions not only spend too much time on outlandish schemes but that some are filled with the addicts of political correctness and left-wing dogma"* (p.55).

Given this kind of view it is easy to be negative about the reforms, and indeed it is true that the changes have brought tension and difficulties between providers. However, it is also true that there are enormous advantages. In particular, because schools and Higher Education Institutions (HEIs) have been required to develop formal partnerships, there are opportunities for staff development in all institutions in collaboration, and this can only be good for the quality of experience which you receive as a trainee teacher.

In considering the framework more closely we will reflect on this idea of partnership in more depth, as it is in the new arrangements that have to be made between schools and HEIs that there is potential for your training to reflect the kind of Environmental Education considered in the following chapters of this book.

It has already been firmly established that there has been a radical shift towards increased school-centred training. This has expression in terms of primary training in DfEE Circular 14/93 mentioned above which, in addition to required competencies, also lays out the principles of partnership and the tasks of partnership. In other words, it provides the principles which are then reflected in formal partnership agreements between institutions. This is important because there is a clear emphasis on the need for integrated professional training where the linkage between schools and HEIs is clearly defined in terms of curriculum content and the development of roles and responsibilities. It is here that there is an ideal opportunity for you to enhance your teaching of Environmental Education because this idea of partnership provides a contrast in which you can teach 'in situ', evaluate your teaching through highly focused professional discourse, and relate these in HEI curriculum courses to wider principles in environmental education. Because partnership requires school and college staff to work together, there is real potential for clear links between Environmental Education in school and HEI to be defined. All this effectively creates a baseline which you can then use as you develop your expertise in teaching:

"The imperative for closer partnership is a welcome opportunity to experiment with new ways of working together. Joint staff development can be a focus for closer collaboration between schools and higher education. From an enhanced relationship, the professional needs and purposes of staff development both in higher education and schools can be jointly articulated, planned, executed and evaluated in the light of common objectives."

GLENNY AND HICKLING, 1995, (P.58)

ENVIRONMENTAL EDUCATION AND PARTNERSHIP IN TEACHER TRAINING

In terms of Environmental Education, the newly emerging partnerships between schools and HEIs offer opportunities to explain the theory and practice of Environmental Education and what later chapters of this book label as 'Education for Sustainability'. The debates about these adjectivals and the purposes of education are now taking place within these new partnerships. We will now consider an example of this actually happening in practice. In the Autumn of 1995, two primary schools in South Cumbria began working with WWF-UK and what is now part of the University College of St Martin to develop understanding of Education for Sustainability, both in terms of whole school development and in working with trainee teachers. During the first year of the project there were a number of key INSET days at which staff from all institutions involved explored the notion of Education for Sustainability, its meaning and application. In-between the INSET days, ongoing curriculum development work was planned which influenced the emergence of new ways of thinking both from College and the schools. This process can be seen in the following example:

Part of the initial work involved much discussion amongst staff about the meaning of Education for Sustainability as a central element of Environmental Education. This was an exciting part of the project and although, rightly, different members of staff had and still have, different views a broad consensus was achieved which was then expressed in actual curriculum work. The consensus reflects Symons' (1996) position that Education for Sustainability needs both critical enquiry and active participation. In terms of the former, she writes: "for real Education for Sustainability to take place, opportunities for critical enquiry must be built into the mainly descriptive and practical nature of such Environmental Education" (p.60). In regard to the latter she mentions that: "sustainable development is dependent on the informal participation of all sections of society and it is essential that experience of democratic processes and thoughtful participation in decision-making and action should start early, and it is a skill that needs practice" (p.61). In the partnership between the schools and the College it began to be recognised that underpinning Education for Sustainability are practical curriculum approaches involving children to undertake enquiry which they own and which they are active in addressing.

This initial work in the partnership was then used further as both schools became directly involved in supporting a block placement. Trainee teachers had opportunities to experience at first hand the development work which had previously occurred in the schools as Education for Sustainability was first defined and then applied. In some cases this led to trainees being able to develop their teaching to reflect the principles of Education for Sustainability. Have a look at the following example:

In one reception class, Kevin used the road play-mat as a focus to encourage children to think about the consequences of increased road usage. The children had been involved in data collection about the mode of transport which class members used to come to school. The survey suggested that many children came to school by car. To illustrate congestion each child was given a toy car to place on the road play-mat. This led to a situation where no child was able to play because there was no space. On asking what could be done to alleviate this situation, a toy bus was used to illustrate the effect that use of public transport could have on reducing congestion and by implication on resource usage.

The point which emerges here is the simplicity of Kevin's style. Here Education for Sustainability did not mean a completely 'different' approach or a radical or marginal concept of teaching. It simply meant being clear about its principles and seeking ways of applying these in an everyday classroom activity. In this way Education for Sustainability is essentially at the centre of good teaching because it involves children being both active and enquiring in their learning; it could well be that it is closer than you think!

The reforms of initial teacher training provide an ideal context for partnership so that HEIs and partner schools have opportunities to develop shared values, in this case to do with Environmental Education and Education for Sustainability. Because of the enhanced role of the school-based mentor as teacher trainer, opportunities are also provided for you to engage in close ongoing professional dialogue with a teacher who has understanding in context of both the principles of Education for Sustainability and also the enactment of these principles in the curriculum and more particularly in teaching processes. In essence school-based mentors are particularly well placed to develop your practice of teaching in Education for Sustainability because they have the role of conducting formal and informal observation and tutorials, through which it is possible to engage in close professional dialogue. This will be enriched if a mentor is already expressing Education for Sustainability in her own teaching processes and who, for example, seeks to enable children to develop their own enquiry and from this an awareness of the implication of their decisions. In these cases professional dialogue between your mentor and yourself based on shared experience of your teaching has enormous potential to challenge both your personal attitudes and values and your expression of these in your own teaching. It is at this level of fine-grain dialogue that your understanding of Education for Sustainability can be enhanced and explored within the real context of a block placement. Put simply it is precisely because of the new national framework for teacher training that there are these opportunities for dialogue with mentors, based on specific classroom activities, and informed through the professional development that has become possible as a result of the wider partnership arrangements in teacher training.

 **OVER TO YOU**

1 Write down three sentences which outline your personal key aims of education.

2 Consider

   a) how you express these aims in your lifestyle, attitudes and values

   b) how you express these aims in your actual teaching

   c) the extent to which these aims link with the central elements of Education for Sustainability.

3 Do you wish to alter any of these aims in the light of Education for Sustainability?

4 Find out what the perspective on Environmental Education is in your placement school. How, if at all, does it link to (a) your personal aims of education and (b) the view of Environmental Education expressed in this book?

5 Does the school have a different view of Environmental Education than the College? Does this matter? What opportunities are there for dialogue?

REFERENCES

Boyson, R, **BOYSON ON EDUCATION,**
Peter Owen, 1996
Clarke, K, Speech given at the 'North of England'
Conference, *1992*
Department for Education and Employment,

**INITIAL TEACHER TRAINING OF
SECONDARY SCHOOL TEACHERS,**
Circular 9/92, *HMSO, 1992*

Department for Education and Employment,
**THE INITIAL TRAINING OF PRIMARY
SCHOOL TEACHERS: NEW CRITERIA FOR
COURSES,** Circular 14/93, *HMSO, 1993*

Glenny and Hickling, *A developmental model of
partnership between primary schools and higher education*
in Bines and Welton, **MANAGING PARTNERSHIP
IN TEACHER TRAINING AND
DEVELOPMENT,** *Routledge, 1995*

Symons, G, **THE PRIMARY YEARS** in Huckle and
Sterling, **EDUCATION FOR SUSTAINABILITY**,
Earthscan, *1996*

Acknowledgements to the staff of Vickerstown and
Pennington primary schools and to Kevin Lawrence
from University College of St Martin

THE WORLD WE HAVE MADE

Crisis? What crisis?

Male fish are being 'feminised' by river pollution

Black market CFCs stall ozone recovery

Western taste for prawns causes third world misery

Why breathing in Britain can be damaging to your health

BSE fears over fourth sick farmer

SELLAFIELD DUMP PLANS FLAWED

These headlines, all from 1995 and '96, tell a sad story. Readers of the so-called 'heavy' papers could not be in much doubt that the world is facing a number of environmental crises (although the tabloids rarely mention them). However, even in the broadsheets they are by no means everyday stories. They appear, often towards the back of the paper, when a new report is published or the European Commission issues a new directive. But days or even weeks go by when nothing of this nature hits the headlines. Unfortunately, this does not mean the problems go away, just that they are not good stories. Only when a major disaster occurs, such as the BSE crisis or the massive oil spill caused by the grounding of the *Sea Empress*, does 'the environment' become newsworthy and achieve top billing.

Environmental issues move up and down the political agenda, according to media coverage, the state of the economy, the demands of the international community and the date of the next elections. The problems also move in and out of people's individual consciousness. We may worry about global warming and dutifully turn the central heating down a degree, but that worry is pushed well down the list if our livelihood is threatened by the closure of the local car factory.

But there is a need for us all to be concerned about these major environmental issues. They are not just the preserve of the pressure groups and NGOs (Non-Governmental Organisations) like WWF, Friends of the Earth and Greenpeace. They are not a few isolated incidents. Look at these facts:

Since the industrial revolution, human numbers have grown eight-fold and industrial production has risen by more than 100 times in the past 100 years. **The 5.3 billion people now on Earth are already using 40% of our most elemental resource – the energy from the sun made available by green plants on land.**

In less than 200 years the planet has lost six million square kilometres of forest; the sediment load from soil erosion has risen three-fold in major river basins and by eight times in smaller, more intensively used ones. Water withdrawals have grown from 100 to 3,600 cubic kilometres a year. **The capacity of the Earth to support human and other life has been significantly diminished.**

Since the mid-eighteenth century, human activities have more than doubled the methane in the atmosphere; increased the concentration of carbon dioxide by 27% and significantly damaged the stratospheric ozone layer. **Atmospheric systems have been disturbed, threatening the climate regime to which we and other forms of life have long been adapted.**

Humanity is causing emissions of arsenic, mercury, nickel and vanadium that are now double those from natural sources; zinc emissions are triple and those from cadmium and lead are respectively five and eighteen times higher than natural rates. **Pollution of air, soil, fresh waters and the oceans has become a serious and continuing threat to the health of humans and other species.**

One person in five cannot get enough food properly to support an active working life. One quarter of the world's people are without safe drinking water. Every year millions of children die from malnutrition and preventable disease. **Such conditions are grossly unjust. They also threaten the peace and stability of many countries now, and of the whole world eventually**.

CARING FOR THE EARTH

We could go on to fill the whole book with frightening statistics and stories of ecological disaster, but that is not our purpose. If you need to be further convinced, there are other books which should do the job.

OVER TO YOU

1 What do you already know about environmental issues?

Do you know the background to any of the stories in those newspaper headlines?

Choose a few of them and jot down what you think the basic story was about.

For example, 'Why breathing in Britain can be damaging to your health'

is obviously about air pollution, and probably about rising asthma rates.

The article could be about vehicle or factory emissions or both.

2 Take one of the stories and think more widely about the issues.

For example, what are the underlying causes?

Might there be a **technological solution** or is a **change in lifestyle** needed?

What would be the **implications** of the various solutions?

Are there any **closely related issues**?

This is not a test; it is a mental exercise.

Try making a web to see where it leads you.

Over the page is one which has been started to give you the idea. You could continue it or start one of your own on a different topic.

You may need a very large piece of paper!

OVER TO YOU

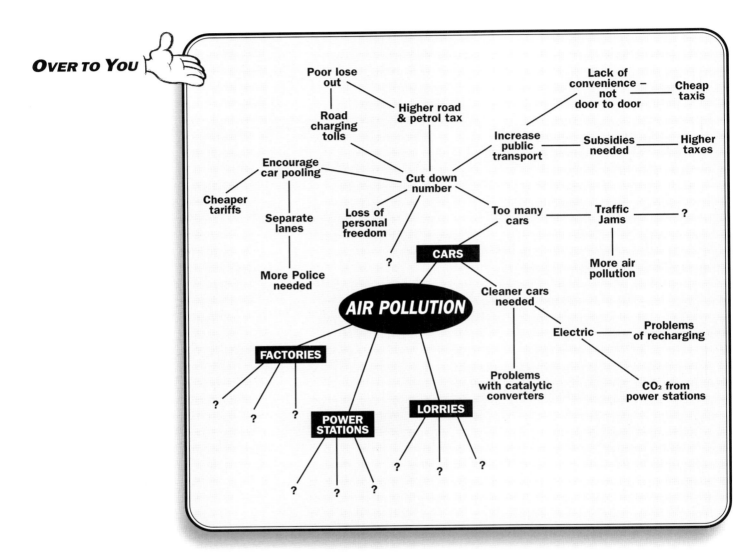

OVER TO YOU

3 Given that you are reading this book at all, you must already have some interest in environmental matters. What has sparked that interest and shaped your ideas?

i Copy the diagram below onto a large sheet of paper. On your own or with a partner write against the line from 'birth' to 'now' any events or developments in your lifetime which have had an impact on the environment.

ii Against the 'probable future' line from 'now' write in key events and trends you think are **likely** to happen which will affect the environment.

iii Against the 'preferred future' line write in events and developments you would **wish** to see happen.

Why is there a difference between the two lines? What sort of changes in people's thinking and governments' actions would be necessary to bring about your preferred future?

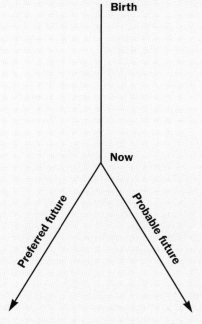

ADAPTED FROM A CENTRE FOR GLOBAL EDUCATION ACTIVITY IN G PIKE AND D SELBY, *GREENING THE STAFFROOM, WWF-UK/CENTRE FOR GLOBAL EDUCATION/BBC EDUCATION, 1990*

*"You think you are
rich, but you wake to
the sound of traffic,
while we wake up
to the sound of our
people singing."*

INDIGENOUS PERSON AT
THE 'EARTH SUMMIT'

OUR OWN BACK YARD

It is quite likely that some of the items you filled in were to do with local issues. The environmental problems that are likely to press on us in the most direct way are probably not those which are planet-threatening, but those which affect the quality of our daily lives – bleak housing estates, crowded trains, littered and dog-fouled streets, noise pollution, excessive road building, air pollution, contaminated water... These are also the problems it may be easiest for us to tackle on a practical level by becoming involved in local politics or action groups – and perhaps by changing our own behaviour.

LOCAL TO GLOBAL

These problems are not unrelated to world issues. There is a continuous scale from local to global. In one street there may be problems with cars parking illegally on pavements; in the town, one in seven children may be suffering from asthma exacerbated by air pollution; in the country, important nature reserves may be concreted over for motorways; half a continent away trees may be dying from acid rain; while globally, the Earth's atmosphere is heating up. The common thread – the motor car.

There are other similar threads of connections, of causes and effects, weaving a net around the globe. Next time you bite into a bar of chocolate, think about this:

*"They'll have to do something
soon. It's affecting polar bears
in the Arctic."*

"The sugar-cane area (in Brazil) is known as the *Zona da Mata* after the great tropical forest, the *Mata Atlantica*, which once covered it. In the seventeenth century the first sugar barons started to clear the forest with the slave labour of the Tupi Indians whose hunting ground it had been. Deforestation continues today. The job is nearly complete; the cane fields now cover almost everything.

'When I was a boy there was still a lot of forest,' Neco remembers... 'Now they've wiped it all out, covered it with cane, but in the forest there used to be a lot of game.' He reels off the names of animals that once boosted the workers' protein intake, and his eyes mist over as he remembers how delicious tatu (armadillo) used to taste...

Today, even plump and tasty *pilapes* fish from the reservoir in front of Neco's house are getting harder to come by; some time ago they began turning up dead on the shore. The fact that a stream flowing into the reservoir was used to wash out barrels of herbicide may have something to do with it."

NEW INTERNATIONALIST

... and this:

> "At least 32 pesticides are used on cocoa plantations...They include Lindane, which is so toxic that one teaspoonful is fatal; Paraquat, a cheap and freely available herbicide that is the most common method of suicide in Malaysia; and Parathion, an organophosphorus insecticide which has been banned in 17 countries including Britain.
>
> These pesticides severely affect the workers who apply them to cocoa crops... Common effects include headaches, nausea and skin rashes. More seriously, contact of the pesticides on the skin may cause severe menstrual problems, reproductive disorders and birth defects in pregnant women."
>
> WOMEN'S ENVIRONMENTAL NETWORK

Other threads include:

Global warming brought about or exacerbated by the burning of fossil fuels; the 'developed' countries use about 40 times as much as the poorer countries but many of the poorer countries of the South are likely to suffer most – higher temperatures and less rainfall in already drought-prone areas, more flooding of low-lying countries like Bangladesh, through rising sea-levels, lack of money to change agricultural practices...

Foreign aid: as a direct consequence of a forest conservation project funded by the European Community, 30,000 Ugandans were displaced from their homes and had to find somewhere new to live.

Multinationals: Pepsico employs 335,000 workers in 100 countries; in London, Ontario, Bendix closed a factory, making 200 workers redundant, and moved the work to plants in southern USA and Mexico.

Debt: 'Third World' (or 'majority world' as they are now sometimes called) countries owe £8,000,000,000 to the UK's big four high street banks. Most are major rainforest countries, including Brazil, Mexico and Venezuela, who are now cutting their forests to grow cash crops and set up industries to help pay their debts.

Toxic waste: in Autumn 1993, 15 container loads of toxic waste, under the guise of soil fertiliser, was shipped from Birmingham to Brazil for disposal. Exposed by Greenpeace, the load was sent back to Britain where, early in 1994, it was still waiting on a quayside in Scunthorpe.

World commodities: wildcat tin mines in Rondonia, Brazil, not only caused devastation in the rainforest but forced the closure of centuries-old mines in Cornwall which could not compete.

You can probably think of many more threads in this ever-tightening net, especially in connection with trade. You only have to look at the shelves in the local supermarket...

"I think the economic logic behind dumping a load of toxic waste in the lowest wage country is impeccable and we should face up to the fact that... underpopulated countries such as Africa are vastly under-polluted."

LAWRENCE SUMMERS, FORMER CHIEF ECONOMIST OF THE WORLD BANK, 1991

"Our horizon no longer stops at the end of the street where we live. We are becoming global citizens, but we do not yet know how to cope with this unaccustomed reality."

HERBERT GIRARDET IN EARTHRISE

HOW DID WE GET INTO THIS FINE MESS?

Environmental problems are not new. The earliest civilisations of Mesopotamia, established in the fertile crescent from Sumeria to Palestine, regarded nature as 'monstrous chaos' to be battled against and brought to order. They built an extensive system of irrigation canals, but did not take into account the rapid evaporation and poor drainage. Salts accumulated in the soil to such an extent that still today it is very difficult to grow crops successfully.

North Africa was once heavily forested, but 2000 years ago it became the breadbasket of ancient Rome. Shiploads of timber were transported to Italy soon followed by huge cargoes of wheat. Years of monoculture and no tree cover led to poor fertility and large-scale soil erosion. The people of the North African deserts are still paying the price.

Two more examples, one even earlier, one more recent, should serve as a warning to us, if only we have ears to hear. About 11,000 years ago there was a fairly sudden disappearance of North American mammoths, mastodons, ground sloths, horses, camels and other large mammals. One theory, by P S Martin, suggests that it is more than chance that this roughly coincides with the appearance of stone-age hunters over the Bering Straits from Siberia. The animals, quite unused to hunters, had no time to build up defensive behaviour and were quickly wiped out.

The final story, about Easter Island, is a classic example of a people outstripping their resources. Thickly wooded when the first Polynesians arrived in about the fifth century, it was almost treeless when the first Europeans visited in 1722. Huge stone statues were evidence of a fairly advanced and leisured civilisation, but the eighteenth century inhabitants were living in squalor and abject poverty. Quite simply, as Clive Ponting relates, they had denuded the island of trees because they cut them down to provide rollers for transporting the huge statues. Soil erosion, loss of fertility and lack of timber for building led to the collapse of society. And they couldn't even escape because they had no trees to build canoes with!

"How do they find their own nests?"

It is easy to see how the planet has reached its current state of crisis. With the world's population having increased from about 250 million in AD 1 to 5.3 *billion* now; with the discovery of fossil fuels; the industrial revolution; the 'green revolution' in agriculture with its heavy reliance

on chemical inputs; our profligate use of non-renewable resources; the inexorable spread of the consumer society where human happiness is measured in material possessions; with our seemingly total disregard for the welfare of people in the poorer countries and generations to come; and with technological advances giving us powers previously only ascribed to the gods, it is no wonder the planet is in a bit of a mess.

AND HOW DO WE GET OUT OF IT?

Everything is not doom and gloom. Some good things are happening; the international community, individual countries, towns and companies are taking certain issues seriously. Sometimes it is a matter of implementing new policies; sometimes applying new technologies; often both. The 1987 Montreal Protocol, for example, set in motion worldwide efforts to halt the thinning of the ozone layer. There is now international agreement to phase out CFCs by the year 2000, and the EC countries have brought forward their date to 1997. In some countries, such as Austria, Australia and the USA, it is illegal not to recover the CFCs from fridges. Nearly all fridges made in Germany are now 'ozone and climate friendly' and China is also converting to the new technology. Scientists predict that recovery of the ozone layer should start around the year 2000 (if nations keep to the Montreal Protocol).

The countries of Western Europe are committed to reducing their emissions of sulphur dioxide (SO_2) and nitrogen oxides (NO_x) by 30–50% before the year 2000, and over 100 major cities have formed the Climate Alliance, pledged to reduce carbon dioxide (CO_2) emissions by 2010.

Other international agreements aim to protect wildlife. The Convention on International Trade in Endangered Species (CITES) lists over 700 species which must not be traded. The International Whaling Commission was able to ban commercial whaling from 1985 (although some countries continue to officially flout the rules, catching whales both for 'scientific' purposes and for sale as meat).

Individual countries are also taking a strong stand on certain issues, particularly on planting new forests. Vietnam, for example, which lost over three-quarters of its forests in the war, has a huge government-led reforestation programme. Eventually it is hoped that every school and every village will have its own tree nursery. Germany has stringent policies on reducing and recycling waste; and Denmark is strongly encouraging wind farms for electricity.

"We are all partners in the destruction of nature, because we all agree to benefit from its spoils."
RANCHOR PRIME

There once was a planet called Earth,
Which gave every life-form its birth,
One called Man, in its greed,
Took far more than its need,
So died out, never knowing its worth.
J SWANN IN
GREAT GREEN LIMERICKS

Some city authorities are forward-looking: Shanghai produces all its own vegetables, fertilised by the waste of the people who live there; Stockholm and Prague grow fruit trees in the streets and public parks; and Leicester, Britain's first 'Environment City', has a whole host of measures to make the city more user-friendly, from traffic-calming measures and new cycleways, through consultancy services for local businesses to its Faith in Nature initiative with the local Hindu community.

Scott, the makers of Andrex, have stopped buying wood pulp from all companies concerned with the destruction of Canadian virgin rainforest in Clayoquot Sound, and many timber users and suppliers have signed up to the Forest Stewardship Council approved wood scheme. Leading supermarkets have started stocking a brand of chocolate made from organic beans, and with a guarantee that a fair price has been paid to the grower...

The commercial world is definitely beginning to wake up both to its environmental responsibilities and to the fact that it can profitably use a 'green' image in marketing. The following advertisement appeared in the broadsheet press, aimed at 'professional specifiers' and people having building work done.

Every time you don't specify wood, you're helping to destroy our planet.

For every tree harvested another can be grown. This is how we achieve sustained yield. And in those soldier-like files of seedlings, there is more than new growth. There is renewed hope for our planet.

As the menacing by-products of our power stations continue to pollute the atmosphere we must reduce our energy consumption. A component made of wood takes less energy to produce than the same in steel, aluminium or concrete. It involves little chemical or toxic waste. Isn't this the way?

Once they're empty, our storehouses of bauxite, iron ore, coal and limestone can never be refilled. A forest, well-managed, is eternal. And whereas young growing trees are the most effective absorbers of CO_2, the production of substitute materials feeds the acid rain that's destroying them.

What then is the key factor in reducing these CO_2 emissions? It seems that only well insulated homes can significantly bring them down. (Currently the energy consumptions of buildings accounts for half our national total demand.)

Just think, if all the houses erected in Britain since World War 2 had conformed to modern timber frame standards, the emissions of over 3,000 million tonnes of CO_2 would have been avoided. It's clear that by growing new trees we are providing the resources of the future.

EXTRACT FROM AN ADVERTISEMENT FROM THE TIMBER TRADES FEDERATION

This advertisement touches on many issues that are crucial to any debate on sustainability and stewardship. How many can you list?

Can you think of any counter-arguments, or any consequences of greater wood consumption which may not be so environment-friendly?

SO IS ALL THIS ENOUGH?

Unfortunately not. Worthy and effective though they all are, these projects are piecemeal answers to specific problems. Technological 'fixes' can help, but do not always deliver their promises and may bring new problems. For example, going back to the problem of air pollution caused by cars: the answer is seen by many to be catalytic converters. Unfortunately, they take several minutes to warm up and start working, and 80% of the harmful gases from a six mile journey are pumped out in the first half mile. Yet 60% of all car journeys are under five miles. What is worse, they actually increase emissions of carbon dioxide, the major 'greenhouse' gas.

"...The problems may be obvious enough, but the solutions are far from evident. One thing is quite certain, we will never be able to break free of the vicious spiral if the leaders in thought and politics persist in the belief that all can be solved by yet more economic development and growth and that all can be put right by some technological fix. I believe that we have got the means to put things right, but they will not be implemented until there is a radical change in attitudes of the opinion-formers. This is easily said, but who is going to start the process of winding down the inter-nation competition for prosperity and better standards of living? Who is going to be the first to face up to the need for self-restraint in the number of children brought into the world? How are the more affluent countries going to be persuaded to drastically reduce their very high demands for natural resources of all kinds? How are the less prosperous countries going to deny themselves the opportunity to exploit some of their natural resources of wildlife, timber and fish when so many of their people depend on them for their livelihood? How else are poverty and deprivation to be relieved? Who is going to start being unselfish for the sake of future generations?"

HRH THE DUKE OF EDINBURGH IN GREENING THE STAFFROOM

The international community has begun to recognise the need for global rethinking and restructuring if the planet and its inhabitants are to be saved. The first international conference on the environment was in Stockholm in 1972, and it led to the creation of UNEP – the United Nations Environment Programme. In the same year the Club of Rome, an international group of thirty influential individuals, published a report called *Limits to Growth*. It investigated five main areas of concern: increasing industrialisation, population growth, widespread malnutrition, depletion of non-renewable resources and a deteriorating environment. It stated clearly that a

"decision to do nothing is a decision to increase the risk of collapse." Little *was* done, partly because the oil crisis of the 1970s slowed down world growth anyway.

In 1980, another major report was published. The IUCN (International Union for Conservation of Nature and Natural Resources), UNEP and WWF published the *World Conservation Strategy*. It stated three main priorities:

- to maintain essential ecological processes and life-support systems
- to preserve genetic diversity
- to sustain utilisation of species and ecosystems.

Although it did put the environment on the international agenda again, it was criticised for being anti-development and anti-poor.

Then in 1982, President Carter of the USA commissioned *Global 2000*, a detailed study of global environmental problems. It painted a very gloomy picture and called on the nations of the world to "act decisively to alter current trends". Sadly, in the boom years of the '80s, subsequent presidents and the rest of the world more or less ignored it.

Probably the most influential publication was *Our Common Future*, the report of The World Commission on Environment and Development, published in 1987. (It is commonly known as the Brundtland Report, after the chair of the commission.)

"If present trends continue, the world in 2000 will be more crowded, more polluted, less stable ecologically, and more vulnerable to disruption than the world we live in now... For hundreds of millions of the desperately poor, the outlook for food and other necessities of life will be no better. For many it will be worse."

GLOBAL 2000

The Brundtland Report
"Two key concepts:

The basic needs of all people must be met in a way which provides for their needs with security and dignity – in the world today, where the needs of so many are not met, this inevitably means giving the poor priority.

There are no absolute limits to development – development potential is a function of the present state of technology and social organisation, combined with their impact on environmental resources.

Seven strategic imperatives:
- reviving economic growth
- changing the quality of growth
- meeting essential needs for jobs, food, energy, water and sanitation
- ensuring a sustainable level of population
- conserving and enhancing the resource base
- reorienting technology and managing risk
- merging environment and economics in decision making"

OUR COMMON FUTURE

THE WORLD WAKES UP

By the late 1980s it was clear that the world was facing unprecedented environmental problems. The United Nations set up the 'Earth Summit', an international Conference on the Environment and Development (UNCED) held in Rio de Janeiro in June 1992. During the build-up to this, IUCN, UNEP and WWF published a new major report, *Caring for the Earth*. Its aims were to:

"...help improve the condition of the world's people by defining two requirements. One is to secure a widespread and deeply held commitment to a new ethic, the ethic for sustainable living, and to translate its principles into practice. The other is to integrate conservation and development to enable people everywhere to enjoy long, healthy and fulfilling lives."

A term used often in *Caring for the Earth* and in many recent speeches, reports and campaign material is 'sustainable development'. There seems to be no real general consensus about what it means and much less about how it is to be achieved. The box below gives an idea of some of its interpretations.

Sustainable development

The first definition, from *Our Common Future*, is the most succinct and well-known. Sustainable development is:

"...development that meets the needs of the present without compromising the ability of future generations to meet their needs."

Birmingham City Council's *Green Action Plan* also emphasises the needs of future generations:

"Sustainability means managing, protecting and conserving the planet's renewable resources, so that, over time, they are regenerated through natural processes or with human intervention to make them available for generations to come, giving them at least the same benefits and opportunities open to us."

Caring for the Earth goes further. One element of a world ethic for living sustainably is:

"Everyone should aim to share fairly the benefits and costs of resource use, among different communities and interest groups, among regions that are poor and those that are affluent, and between present and future generations. Each generation should leave to the future a world that is at least as diverse and productive as the one it inherited. Development of one society or generation should not limit the opportunities of other societies or generations."

The Earth Summit in Rio was the largest-ever gathering of world leaders. This in itself was an achievement and provided an opportunity to educate these leaders and opinion formers in environmental issues. A huge parallel forum of Non-Governmental Organisations (NGOs), community groups and indigenous peoples helped to keep vital issues in the media spotlight.

Many criticisms of the conference were voiced before, during and after the event. There were conventions on climate, biodiversity and forests, but not on debt, free trade, transnationals or consumption levels – all of which were wanted by the poorer countries of the world. With a few exceptions, the richer nations offered little new money to the poorer countries which they desperately need to help them develop in a sustainable way. Big business made few concessions to environmental regulation and concentrated rather on securing their access to the resources of the South.

However, at the end, there were a number of positive measures including the endorsing of *Agenda 21*, a comprehensive blueprint for the global actions needed to affect the transition to sustainable development, and the signing of two legally binding treaties on biodiversity and climate change.

The British Government had already produced a White Paper on environment and development in 1990, *This Common Inheritance*, and has since published its official responses to *Agenda 21*, *Sustainable Development: The UK Strategy*. It proposed the setting up of an independent panel of experts to advise on policy; a Round Table on sustainable development to co-ordinate local government, business and other interests; a 'Going for Green' campaign, and some suggestions for energy efficiency, fuel and road taxes, marine conservation and water metering.

"The United Kingdom is determined to make sustainable development the touchstone of its policies... The Government is committed to pursuing development for the UK in a way which promotes the sustainable development of the world as a whole."

Sustainable Development: The UK Strategy

So that's all right then?

Once again the answer, inescapably, is 'no'. The Government's strategy has come in for a lot of criticism, largely on account of what it does *not* say, rather than what it does. Many of the policies were not new and there was little about the crucial issues of road building, rail and forestry privatisation or nuclear power. It talked a great deal about market forces, voluntary agreements and technological solutions, but very little about community- and people-centred initiatives or new moral standards and an ethic of sharing. Critics accuse the document of having no co-ordinated vision and no sense of urgency and some would also argue that there is little evidence the Government is commited to carrying out what it has signed up to.

It is quite true that the Government cannot do everything. We are all responsible; it really is a case of 'if we are not part of the solution, we are part of the problem'. As individuals we need to change our own lifestyles, cut down our energy consumption, compost our vegetable waste, refuse excess packaging and make 'green' consumer choices, (as *The UK Strategy* stresses*)*.

But this is not enough either. These sorts of changes are easy to make. To have any greater effect, people need to join together. *Caring for the Earth* emphasises throughout that if we are to achieve sustainability, communities must be empowered to care for their own environments. We must care about our immediate locality enough to want to make it a pleasant and viable place to live, and we must also care about the wider community. After all, the word 'community' itself can embrace almost any size and type of group from a few families living co-operatively in a large shared house to the huge and anonymous European Community. One of the early slogans of the 'green' movement was "think global, act local". This still holds true, but perhaps it is no longer enough. We must certainly 'act local' but at the same time we must make sure our leaders 'act global' on our behalf.

Caring for the Earth suggests nine principles for a sustainable world society:
- respect and care for the community of life
- improve the quality of life
- conserve the Earth's vitality and diversity
- minimise the depletion of non-renewable resources
- keep within the Earth's carrying capacity
- change personal attitudes and practices
- enable communities to care for their own environments
- provide a national framework for integrating development and conservation
- create a global alliance.

"The market is the most effective mechanism for maintaining the momentum of development, sharing its benefits, and for shaping its course towards sustainability."

SUSTAINABLE DEVELOPMENT:
THE UK STRATEGY

"Never doubt that a small group of committed citizens can change the world, indeed it is the only thing that ever has."

MARGARET MEAD, SOCIAL
ANTHROPOLOGIST

"A human being is a part of the whole called by us the universe... She or he can experience herself or himself... as something separated from the rest, a kind of separation-delusion of her or his consciousness. This delusion can be a kind of prison for us, restricting us to our personal desires and to affection for a few persons nearest to us. Our task must be to free ourselves... by widening our circle of compassion to embrace all living creatures and the whole of nature in all its beauty."

ALBERT EINSTEIN

OVER TO YOU

What do you think?

On the following pages are some opinions about the relationship between humans and the environment and how we can best solve the global problems we have caused. To what extent do you agree with them?

You can do this activity on your own, but it would be more valuable to do it with a friend. There are no right answers – it is the thinking and discussion which are important. You will probably need to negotiate with your partner to achieve a ranking you both agree on. If you are doing it on your own, try ranking the cards in different ways, and seeing if you can make justifications for the different orders.

1 *Photocopy the page opposite. Cut up the cards.*

2 *Place them in a diamond shape according to how far you agree with them.*
   The statement you think is most significant is placed at the top of the diamond. The next three are placed in second equal position. The four across the centre are fifth equal, the next three ninth equal and the one at the foot of the diamond is the one you least agree with.

```
                1
          2     2     2
       5     5     5     5
          9     9     9
                12
```

Was it easy to pick out one which most nearly represents your view? Could you expand on it if you had to justify it in a discussion?

Was there one you strongly disagreed with? Why? What sort of person or group might hold such an opinion?

Are some of the statements totally incompatable or is there 'a little truth' in all of them?

What do you think is the point of this activity?

SOURCE: G PIKE AND D SELBY, *GREENING THE STAFFROOM*, WWF-UK/CENTRE FOR GLOBAL EDUCATION/BBC EDUCATION, 1990, *BASED ON AN IDEA IN* R RICHARDSON AND S FISHER, *DEBATE AND DECISION*, WORLD STUDIES PROJECT, 1980

KING OF THE SPECIES

I don't subscribe to the 'gloom and doom' approach. Whenever we've had some 'global crisis' in the past, we've discovered ways in which to handle it. That's why homo sapiens is the king of the species.

LEAVE IT TO NATURE

Let us not get carried away by the supposed 'gravity' of the problem. Of course we have done a lot of damage to our environment, but the natural world is wonderfully renewable. As long as we control excessive damage and destruction, we can leave it all to nature.

IT'S OUR EARTH

Environmental action provides one of the few remaining arenas for direct participation by ordinary people. We need to grasp the opportunity to defend our natural environment from the insensitivity of politicans and bureaucrats. It's our Earth — we must now assume responsibility for saving it.

GREEN REVOLUTION

There will always be an environmental crisis whilst we have a consumer society, fostered by both capitalism and state socialism. We need a radical and fundamental change in outlook and in economic and social relations. Nothing short of a 'dark green' revolution in our personal lives and in society at large will suffice.

DAY-TO-DAY SURVIVAL

It's all very well for the 'Rich North' to go on about global warming, the threat to the ozone layer, conservation and so on. In the 'Poor South' survival of the planet is the least of our worries. It's day-to-day survival that concerns us most.

MALE VALUES

At the root of most environmental problems is the philosophy of dominance or control over nature; this is hardly surprising in a world in which male values are predominant. Effective long-term solutions require a radical re-thinking of our relationship to the natural world — a commitment to the female values of nurturing, harmony and peaceful co-existence.

Source: G Pike and D Selby, Greening the Staffroom, WWF-UK/Centre for Global Education/BBC Education, 1990, based on an idea in R Richardson and S Fisher, Debate and Decision, World Studies Project, 1980

GREEN CONSUMER

The new breed of green consumer is leading the way. We are demanding more information about the environmental effects of products, about the use of animal testing, about the implications for the Third World. We want to know the story behind what we buy. As consumers, we have real power to effect change. And we can use our ultimate power, voting with our feet and wallets – either buying a product somewhere else or not buying it at all.

ENVIRONMENTAL ECONOMICS

The basic problem is that most of our environmental problems result from the misuse of natural resources and services. The environment is often treated as a free 'sink' for wastes and this results in such problems as marine pollution and global warming. We should alter the way in which individuals, firms and governments have to do their economic accounting. If prices and other economic indicators reflected the real environmental costs of products and polices, we would soon realise sustainable development.

RIGHTS

'The environment' is a Western concept: each society, each culture has a right to use its natural surroundings according to its own religious and moral codes and values and its own social and economic needs. No group of people, however affluent or powerful, should dictate to others how their environment is to be used.

ENVIRONMENTAL POLITICS

The basic problem is that our major political parties are too interested in propping up a non-sustainable economy and keeping the voters happy in the short term. The environment is generally low down on their agenda and is treated in a piecemeal, superficial and pragmatic way. We need government by a party which makes sustainable development its priority and legislates to bring about a national programme to integrate development and conservation.

NO SIMPLE ANSWERS

We need to understand that there are no simple answers to environmental problems. In the interdependent · world system, all solutions will have repercussions, beneficial and adverse, on the lifestyles of people somewhere in the world. It's all a matter of choice – difficult choices to be made according to what we hold most dear.

EDUCATION

The basic problem is that current forms of education maintain non-sustainable forms of development. They are part of the problem not the solution. If education is to assist the transition to sustainable development it must challenge prevailing ways of living with nature or existing economic, political and cultural realities. It should adopt an holistic philosophy which recognises our essential connectedness with everything and everyone else. Only then will it be able to educate the whole person to live at peace with the whole planet.

Source: G Pike and D Selby, Greening the Staffroom, WWF-UK/Centre for Global Education/BBC Education, 1990, based on an idea in R Richardson and S Fisher, Debate and Decision, World Studies Project, 1980

References

PLEISTOCENE EXTINCTIONS:
THE SEARCH FOR A CAUSE
P S Martin and H E Wright Jr (eds),
Yale University Press, 1967

A GREEN HISTORY OF THE WORLD
Clive Ponting, Sinclair Stevenson, 1991
and Penguin Books, 1992

CARING FOR THE EARTH
IUCN/UNEP/WWF, 1991

NEW INTERNATIONALIST
Alex Shankland, November 1991

NEWSLETTER NO. 22
Women's Environmental Network, Spring 1994

EARTHRISE
Herbert Girardet, Paladin, 1992

GREAT GREEN LIMERICKS
W H Allen, 1989

GREENING THE STAFFROOM
G Pike and D Selby, WWF-UK/Centre for Global
Education/BBC Education, 1990

LIMITS TO GROWTH: a Report for The Club of
Rome on the Predicament of Mankind
Donella H Meadows et al, Earth Island, 1972

WORLD CONSERVATION STRATEGY
IUCN/UNEP/WWF, 1980

Global 2000

OUR COMMON FUTURE
WCED, Oxford University Press, 1987

GREEN ACTION PLAN, *p6*
Birmingham City Council,

AGENDA 21: THE UNITED NATIONS
PROGRAMME OF ACTION FROM RIO
UN Department of Public Information, 1993

THIS COMMON INHERITANCE:
THE FIRST YEAR REPORT
HMSO, 1991

SUSTAINABLE DEVELOPMENT:
THE UK STRATEGY
HMSO, 1994

THE NEED FOR ENVIRONMENTAL EDUCATION

> "It is essential if environmental policies are to achieve their objective, that there is wide public awareness of the issues at stake and their importance to the future of the planet and future generations. Education has an essential part to play..."
>
> THIS COMMON INHERITANCE: BRITAIN'S ENVIRONMENTAL STRATEGY, HM GOVERNMENT, HMSO, 1990
>
> "We recognise that this [sustainable development] means a change of attitudes throughout the nation. ...Sustainable development requires changes in lifestyles from everyone."
>
> SUSTAINABLE DEVELOPMENT: THE UK STRATEGY, HM GOVERNMENT, HMSO, 1994

These two principles, enshrined in Government policy, could be seen as the main strands of Environmental Education today: awareness of the issues and the changing of attitudes and lifestyles.

This hasn't always been the case. Some form of Environmental Education has always been on the school timetable, but in the early days it was mostly teaching *about* the natural world; it would come under the heading of Nature Study, Geography, Biology, Rural Studies... Later, teachers started to recognise that the local environment was an ideal resource *through* which other subjects and skills could be taught in a way that was direct and relevant for the children. In the '60s and '70s the urban studies movement stressed that children could become involved in local issues, that they could make changes in their own school and grounds and begin to care *for* the environment themselves.

The three words in italics have long been the cornerstones of the Environmental Education movement: education *about* the environment, education *through* the environment and education *for* the environment. The three classifications are still valid and useful. They were used in the original National Curriculum Council policy for Environmental Education as spelled out in *Curriculum Guidance 7* and have been repeated in *Teaching Environmental Matters through the National Curriculum*, published by SCAA in 1996 at the request of the Government.

However, times and the world's problems have moved on, and the emphasis both in educational circles and the world at large is shifting more and more to education *for* the environment, but with some new slants and new urgencies. In the 1980s those involved in Environmental Education and those in Development Education began to come together, realising that they were two sides of the same coin. At the same time there were a number of high-level intergovernmental conferences on Environmental Education organised by branches of the United Nations which stressed both education for sustainable development and teacher training in Environmental Education. In 1990 the United Nations produced a report called *Children and the Environment* which raised issues of justice between generations, local-global links, children's perspectives and 'empowerment and critical awareness'. In 1992, 3,000 delegates from all over the world met at the World Congress for Education and Communication to discuss sustainable development. *Agenda 21* (from the 'Earth Summit' in 1992) which the UK Government signed, stresses "participation and empowerment" of the people and states that education must develop people's abilities as decision makers.

In the box on the opposite page are some quotations from these and other documents setting out what Environmental Education should be doing now. What is significant is the growing use of the term 'education for sustainability', growing out of the increasing need to challenge conventional wisdoms and models of social, economic and political organisation. What is rather strange is that given HM Government's supposed commitment to EE, its major 1994 policy document on sustainable development doesn't mention environmental education as a cross-curricular theme; and the 1994 report to the Government on the reform of the National Curriculum (by Sir Ron Dearing) mentions the environment only in passing.

OVER TO YOU

The quotations opposite are all small excerpts from much longer documents, so judgements and comparisons cannot be made about their overall intentions or focuses. However, there are some common threads in these various declarations and aims. What do you think they are? How do their emphases differ? For example:

Do some seem to focus on environmental management and control, while others stress change in attitudes?

Do some lay more emphasis on justice between societies than others?

Do any seem to be proposing a radical new world order?

Are some more general than others? Is there any advantage in being more 'precise'?

Do any of them seem to omit elements you would consider vital?

Which do you find most helpful?

While you are thinking about these questions, have a look also at the two lists of aims at the beginning of the next chapter and see how they compare.

Environmental Education

"The goals of Environmental Education:

a) to foster clear awareness of, and concern about, economic, political and ecological interdependence in urban and rural areas;

b) to provide every person with opportunities to acquire the knowledge, values, attitudes, commitment and skills needed to protect and improve the environment;

c) to create new patterns of behaviour of individuals, groups and society as a whole towards the environment."

TBILISI RECOMMENDATIONS, 1978 (A UNITED NATIONS INTERGOVERNMENTAL CONFERENCE)

"Learning for Living means growing up to take responsibility for one's own learning and the quality of one's environment, with an increasing awareness of obligations to others and to the natural world. A constructive environmental policy backed by a balanced educational programme aimed to foster environmental competence, to identify the health of one's environment with one's own health, to encourage national participation in the development for all of a sustainable life-style, for the future as well as for the present, this is the policy we must continue to work for."

LEARNING FOR LIVING, SCOTTISH ENVIRONMENTAL EDUCATION COUNCIL, 1985

"The objective of environmental education is to increase the public awareness of the problems in this field, as well as the possible solutions, and to lay the foundations for a fully informed and active participation of the individual in the protection of the environment and the prudent and rational use of natural resources."

EUROPEAN COMMUNITY RESOLUTION OF THE COUNCIL AND MINISTERS OF EDUCATION, 1988

"Education is critical for promoting sustainable development and improving the capacity of the people to address environment and development issues... it is critical for achieving environmental and ethical awareness, values and attitudes, skills and behaviour consistent with sustainable development and for effective participation in decision making."

AGENDA 21, 1992 (FROM THE EARTH SUMMIT IN RIO DE JANEIRO)

"We consider that environmental education for equitable sustainability is a continuous learning process based on a respect for life. Such education affirms values and actions which contribute to human and social transformation and ecological preservation. It fosters ecologically sound and equitable societies that live together in interdependence and diversity. This requires individual and collective responsibility at local, national and planetary levels."

ALTERNATIVE TREATIES FROM THE INTERNATIONAL NGO FORUM, RIO DE JANEIRO, 1992

"Education for sustainability is a process which:

• enables people to understand the interdependence of all life on this planet and the repercussions that their actions and decisions may have both now and in the future on resources, on the global community as well as their local one, and on the total environment;

• increases people's awareness of the economic, political, cultural, technological and environmental forces which foster or impede sustainable development;

• develops people's awareness, competence, attitudes and values, enabling them to be effectively involved in sustainable development at local, national and international levels, and helping them to work towards a more equitable and sustainable future. In particular, it enables people to integrate environmental and economic decision making."

GOOD EARTHKEEPING, EDUCATION FOR SUSTAINABILITY FORUM, UNEP-UK, 1992

ENVIRONMENTAL EDUCATION IN THE CLASSROOM

"Environmental Education aims to:

- *provide opportunities to acquire the knowledge, values, attitudes, commitment and skills needed to protect and improve the environment.*

- *encourage pupils to examine and interpret the environment from a variety of perspectives – physical, geographical, biological, sociological, economic, political, technological, historical, aesthetic, ethical and spiritual.*

- *arouse pupils' awareness and curiosity about the environment and encourage active participation in resolving environmental problems."*

CURRICULUM GUIDANCE 7

The goals of Environmental Education:

- *to foster clear awareness of, and concerns about, economic, political and ecological interdependence.*

- *to provide every young person with opportunities to develop knowledge, values, attitudes, commitment and skills needed to protect and improve the environment and achieve more sustainable forms of human development.*

- *to encourage the emergence of responsible patterns of behaviour towards the environment by individuals and communities."*

ENVIRONMENTAL EDUCATION:
A FRAMEWORK FOR THE DEVELOPMENT OF A CROSS-CURRICULAR THEME IN WALES, ADVISORY PAPER 17

Although these two documents were not reissued with the Revised National Curriculum, they are still operational and state the Government's suggestions for schools on the subject of Environmental Education. In this chapter we hope to illustrate just how they can become a vital part of your teaching and how you can build on them to practise real education for sustainability. You may feel, as we do, that it is much easier to be the person who writes the high-minded statements than the person who has to implement them. How do you work towards "global rethinking and restructuring" with a lively class of seven-year-olds on a wet afternoon?

It need not be such a daunting prospect. There are plenty of useful resources to provide you with the 'what' and also, just as importantly, with the 'how'. For if we are concerned as much with attitudes as with knowledge, then our choice of teaching styles and learning opportunities will be significant. By the end of this chapter, we hope you will have a clearer idea of how to practise Environmental Education. And the following chapters will provide even more help with some model topics and lesson plans.

THE GOVERNMENT'S VIEW ON ENVIRONMENTAL EDUCATION

As already discussed, the report on the revisions of the National Curriculum by Sir Ron Dearing (in early 1994) made no mention of Environmental Education by name, but in the section headed "The Educational Challenge", Sir Ron placed an emphasis on an understanding of education that is not totally subject-based:

"Education is not concerned only with equipping students with the knowledge and skills they need for earning a living. It must help our young people to: use leisure time creatively; have respect for other people, other cultures and other beliefs; become good citizens; think things out for themselves; pursue a healthy lifestyle; and, not least, value themselves and their achievements. It should develop an appreciation of the richness of our cultural heritage and of the spiritual and moral dimensions to life. It must, moreover, be concerned to serve all our children well, whatever their background, sex, creed, ethnicity or talent."

SIR RON DEARING, THE NATIONAL CURRICULUM AND ITS ASSESSMENT, PARA. 3.11

To this end, he recommended that the subject matter of the National Curriculum should be reduced by 20% as from 1995. This should provide time for schools to nurture children as well as teach them knowledge. As Dearing says, in the paragraph that comes closest to mentioning Environmental Education:

"The National Curriculum was never intended to occupy the whole of the school time. The prevailing view when the Education Reform Bill was before Parliament was that it should occupy some 70-80%, leaving the balance for use at the discretion of the school. A margin for use at the discretion of the school is needed in the interests of providing the best possible education. It provides scope for the school to draw upon particular strengths in its teaching staff; to take advantage of learning opportunities provided by the local environment; and to respond to the needs and enthusiasms of particular children."

IBID, PARA. 3.2

In 1996, the School Curriculum and Assessment Authority published a new guidance document, *Teaching Environmental Matters through the National Curriculum*, at the request of the Government. However, it makes clear that the statutory obligation is learning *about* environmental issues, as the very title suggests. Although the document still mentions education *through* and *for* the environment, it clearly states: "...the phrase 'education about the environment' is used throughout the text". It also says that it is for schools to decide whether, and if so to what extent, they wish to develop work in this area beyond their statutory obligation. It is also perhaps significant that the words 'values', 'attitudes' and 'commitment' have been deleted from the aims as originally published in *Curriculum Guidance 7*, although it is encouraging that the term 'sustainable development' is one of the issues now to be engaged with. More recent encouragement comes in the form of the Government Strategy for Environmental Education in England, the stated objective being: "...to instill in people of all ages, through formal and informal education, and training, the concepts of sustainable development and responsible global citizenship...". Most of this book was written before the appearance of the SCAA document and new Government strategy document, but *CG7* remains a key text.

FOCUS ON SCHOOLS

Every school is different. It is constantly surprising how primary schools can vary. Even schools that are barely half a mile apart can have totally different organisations, atmospheres, strengths and weaknesses. Some schools may have Environmental Education policies and a member of staff with a responsibility allowance for this area; other schools may barely mention Environmental Education in their documents. The National Curriculum may be common to all, but its implementation, even before the freeing of the timetable that Dearing recommended, is entirely up to the school and its governors.

When you next get to know a school reasonably well, either by visiting for a number of days or by being on teaching practice for a few weeks, review the ways in which the school shows awareness of Environmental Education. These headings may help you:

1 **Aims of the school:** Schools often have a document with this rather grand title in which they proclaim that they celebrate difference, value everybody's contribution, care for the whole community and seek to develop citizens for tomorrow. Look for evidence that a school has really thought these aims through and developed learning opportunities that foster caring, independence of thought or the building of a critical faculty.

2   **Management of the school and its grounds:** It is always interesting to see what schools have done with their surroundings. The most unpromising are sometimes turned into havens of delight; some remain stubbornly unfriendly, sullen asphalt rectangles that somehow invite rowdy and bullying behaviour at playtime. Look as well at the quality of displays in the entrance hall and the corridors and try to assess the atmosphere of the school. While you make this critical appraisal, try also to think of how you would set about improving things. This is an important part of the exercise because it is all too easy to be judgemental, and much harder to be constructively critical.

3   **Caring for the school environment:** Themes for school assemblies, work outside the classrooms, and attitudes expected from the children should give you an idea of how the 'hidden curriculum' contributes to Environmental Education.

4   **Communication and links with the community:** Does the school operate in a vacuum or does it open its doors to outside influences? Are the children playing a part in debating local issues or implementing local initiatives? Are there any visitors around apart from you?

5   **The curriculum:** It is difficult to get a broad overview of a school's curriculum when you are just visiting a class. However, by questioning the head and teachers, and having a look at the school's long-term planning, it may be possible to identify where and how Environmental Education is taught.

FOCUS ON TEACHERS (THAT MEANS YOU)

Before we move into the classroom to consider the teaching and learning that can be associated with Environmental Education, let us put the spotlight on teachers. When you are beginning your classroom experience it is very common to feel unskilled and inadequate. It helps if you can try to be objective and assess your own strengths and needs. The subjects you enjoyed at school may now have become your hobbies. Perhaps it was when you left school that you found an enthusiasm. If you have degree subjects you may want to continue exploring them, or you may be glad to have finished with them. Whatever your interests, sports, crafts, the arts, nature, history, gardening, they all bring with them certain skills and methods of study. For example, any art or craft activity will have taught you to look after your materials and to work tidily. Any natural history hobby will have taught you to be patient, to observe closely, to make careful notes. Don't dismiss these skills as 'only hobbies' because they will all be useful to you as a teacher. You may already have more 'competencies' than you realise (see below).

And what of your needs? Again, it is worth while considering them, because no primary teacher can duck out of teaching a subject because they consider themselves 'hopeless'. Getting to grips with a subject in order to teach it can actually be fun. Much of the knowledge component of Environmental Education is already in the Geography, Science and, to some extent, History curriculum. The books and other materials that are produced nowadays are much more 'user friendly' than the text books you may remember. Exciting and innovative ways of teaching the necessary knowledge, skills and attitudes can be found in the resource packs currently available from non-mainstream publishers. There is a list at the end of this book.

A relatively new concept in teacher education is the idea of competencies. Rather like the Citizen's Charter, its first appearance is hopeful and stimulating, yet somehow it promises more of a solution than it can ever deliver. The idea is to list all the attributes of a successful teacher, make sure that they are all taught during the teaching course and assess how many the student has achieved at the end of the course. If only it were so simple! However, the idea of making a list is a good way of focusing on a subject. When the teaching of Environmental Education was explored in this way, a list of competencies was drawn up by UNESCO-UNEP, 1990.

Here is a brief summary of the main points of the five categories that were identified:

1   An understanding of the concepts, principles and knowledge of ecology.

2   An understanding of socio-political structures and the interdependence of people and nature; an ability to analyse environmental issues and assess their social implications; and an understanding of the value assumptions behind alternative meanings of sustainable development.

3   Investigation and evaluation skills necessary to work with data and formulate alternative solutions; the ability to analyse their own attitudes and change their position when appropriate.

4   A selection of environmental action skills, enabling the teacher to be willing and competent to take positive action to protect the quality of life.

5   The professional competencies that enable teachers to effectively implement appropriate methodologies in their teaching. These include: interdisciplinary, outdoor education and field-work, critical thinking and enquiry learning, values education, simulations, case-study approaches, community-based learning, investigation of local issues and evaluation in environmental problem solving.

If you bear these categories in mind, it is easier to train yourself to be critically reflective in your teaching. This habit comes naturally to some students; others approach their teaching in a more intuitive way, and cannot analyse their performance without guidance from a mentor. Reflecting on the teaching of a session is just as important as reflecting on the learning that has taken place. Certainly you need to check on whether your objectives have been achieved, but might you have been conveying any hidden messages? Was the style of the session/project suited to the content? Did you encourage thinking in the children? In what ways were you educating *for* the environment?

"One of the principal functions of education is to prepare students for the active discharge of the responsibilities of citizenship. So issues of a politically controversial character will figure by design in some parts of the curriculum and can arrive spontaneously in others."

THE TREATMENT OF
POLITICALLY CONTROVERSIAL
ISSUES IN SCHOOLS

FOCUS ON THE CLASSROOMS

We now come to the crucial part of this chapter in which the 'how' of Environmental Education is put under the microscope. It might be advisable to give a mild word of warning at this point. We must recognise that Environmental Education for sustainable development is a socially critical form of education, and it must be handled sensitively. You may have been changing your opinions and habits as you realise the plight of the planet, maybe becoming a vegetarian, using your bicycle more or joining a protest demonstration; education for sustainable development invites children to consider their own attitudes and behaviour.

Agenda 21, endorsed by world leaders at Rio de Janeiro in June 1992, as part of its key focus on education, encourages in children the sense of 'empowerment', so that they will feel that they have not only the right but the responsibility to organise and act. If we are trying to educate for sustainability then we are necessarily trying to change society, or the society of the future, and we have to be prepared to justify what we are doing. Parents may understandably object to children coming home and telling them that their lifestyles and even the ethics of society are wrong. Teachers of primary children have to sow seeds rather than didactically preach about a new world order. It is from the manner of teaching as much as the matters taught that children will adopt caring attitudes of responsible stewardship.

Nevertheless, it is important that even young children are encouraged to discuss controversial issues at their own level. The role of the teacher is to provide facts (both by 'telling' and by providing resources); to help children formulate their ideas and express them confidently; to value each child's contribution (although it should be made clear that racist and sexist remarks will not be tolerated); to encourage children to listen to and consider the opinions of others; to make clear that changing one's mind in the light of new evidence or a persuasive argument is a positive step, not a climb-down; to put alternative points of view or gentle challenges if the discussions seems too one-sided and to correct facts which are patently incorrect.

This may sound a bit daunting, but it is really just a matter of comments such as:

"That's a good point you've made, but how does it fit with Carmel's idea about..."

"You've put your argument very clearly but I'm afraid your figures for.... are not right. According to .... they are ...."

"You all seem to agree with that, but how would you answer someone who said...."

"That's a good solution for the visitors, but what about the people who live there?"

(A good way of encouraging children to consider all sides of an argument without having to commit themselves is through role play, where they speak with the voice of someone directly involved in, or affected by, an issue.)

Many of the facts about environmental crises are potentially very frightening. It would be misguided, if not wrong, to paint appalling pictures of the end of the world. But children can be helped, for example, to see the sense in reducing car use by reference to air pollution, traffic jams and danger to pedestrians, rather than by suggesting that their home town is in imminent danger of being destroyed by floods from melting ice-caps brought about by global warming.

If we return to *Curriculum Guidance 7* as a basis for teaching, we can look in detail at the three aims and how they can be implemented. The diagram over the page tries to link the theoretical with the practical. Topics 1,2 and 3 refer to the three topics covered later in this book.

The primary years provide the ideal time to interest children in the environment. Environmental Education can provide so many enjoyable and thought-provoking experiences that it is worth considering how you can teach it as well as possible.

"Teachers who adopt an active-learning and person-respecting model of education are committed to creating an environment in which opinions will not be confused with 'final answers', even by the very young. ...Deciding not to teach about controversial issues can be a way of perpetuating inequality and injustice."

MAKING GLOBAL CONNECTIONS

The 3 aims for Environment

Promoting positive attitudes to the environment is essential if pupils are to value it and understand their role in safeguarding it for the future. Encouraging the development of attitudes and personal qualities listed below will contribute to this process:

Why

Aim 1
Provide opportunities to acquire the <u>knowledge</u>, <u>values</u>, <u>attitudes</u>, <u>commitment</u> and <u>skills</u> needed to protect and improve the environment.

Wh

- appreciation of, and care and concern for the environment and for other living things
- independence of thought on environmental issues
- a respect for the beliefs and opinions of others
- a respect for evidence and rational argument tolerance and open-mindedness.

CG 7, p6

Ho

Aim 2
Encourage pupils to examine and interpret the environment from a variety of perspectives – physical, geographical, biological, sociological, economic, political, technological, historical, aesthetic, ethical and spiritual.

e.g. roads, see Topic 2

e.g. growing crops, see Topic 3

e.g. tourism, see Topic 2

e.g. environmentally friendly transport, see Topic 2

e.g. poetry, see Topic 1

e.g. homes around the world, see Topic 1

e.g. families, see Topic 1

e.g. food, see Topic 3

e.g. transport, see Topic 2

e.g. tourism, see Topic 2

e.g. family love, see Topic 1

ducation in Curriculum Guidance 7

- the natural processes which take place in the environment
- the impact of human activities on the environment
- environmental issues such as the greenhouse effect, acid rain, air pollution
→ - local, national and international legislative controls to protect and manage the environment; how policies and decisions are made
- the environmental interdependence of individuals, groups, communities, and nations
- how human lives and livelihoods are dependent on the environment
- the conflicts which can arise about environmental issues
- how the environment has been affected by past decisions and actions
- the importance of planning and design and aesthetic considerations
- the importance of effective action to protect and manage the environment."

CG 7, p4

Communication skills: expressing views and ideas about the environment through different media: arguing clearly and concisely
Numeracy skills: collecting, classifying and analysing data
Study skills: retrieving, analysing, interpreting and evaluating information from a variety f sources
Problem-solving skills: identifying causes and consequences environmental problems; forming reasoned opinions and developing balanced judgements
Personal and social skills: working co-operatively with others, taking individual and group responsibility for the environment
Information technology skills: collecting information and entering it into a data base; simulating an invetigation using IT."

CG7, p6

im 3		
rouse pupils' vareness d curiosity pout the vironment d encourage tive rticipation in solving vironmental oblems.	By	Implementing this aim might include any of the following: Participatory learning Co-operative learning Enquiry-based approach Opportunities for action and problem solving (real or simulations) Opportunities for discussing views and beliefs Positive approach to the environment First-hand experiences Links with the local community Use of real-life issues Use of secondary sources A variety of approaches to teaching and learning.

Planning and Evaluation of Environmental Education, Christiane Dorion, WWF-UK

PART 5

There are many models of planning that can help you:

The environment as a topic itself. The National Curriculum for Geography has 'environment' as one of the themes which must be studied. In Key Stage 2 the wording suggests that issues of management and protection are investigated, which implies that children will be questioning and making decisions as well as just learning facts. Teachers can ask why some environments are in danger, how they can be protected, who is involved and what are the social implications of any proposed protection measures. There should also be a place for discussing the ideas of sustainability; how we could have avoided getting into such an environmental mess in the past, and how we can avoid it in the future with changes of attitude and, perhaps, of social systems. This is the kind of teaching that is the key to effective Environmental Education (see, for example, the 'Tropical Beach Hotel' activity in the Journeys topic later in the book).

Environmental Education as part of a wider topic. In the topic in this book on 'My home, my street', the environment is not the main focus, but it is specifically written in as an element in the topic plan. Also, by choosing teaching methods and class organisation that emphasise co-operation and empathy with other people, a teacher can bring an environmental aspect to any topic. Again, in 'My home, my street' there is a session plan which explains a group game. Ideas of the basic human needs for living are taught, and at the same time the children are learning to co-operate in joint decision-making. Another session which looks at house-building materials is extended to consider where the materials come from. The teacher could then help the children begin to understand the significance of the quarries and pits they see in the landscape, and to think about the future use of such pits.

Environmental Education as a linking element in a theme. In the 'Journeys' topic, for example, both the Geography and History cover the National Curriculum requirements, but there is also an environmental theme running through the topic, helping to unify it. This usefully shows children that the world is not divided into school subjects; History and Geography are inseparably linked. What people did in the past affects the landscape today; our decisions to build a dam today is history tomorrow.

Environmental Education incidentally. A teacher may well find ways of bringing an environmental or sustainability aspect into a topic. In the 'Food' topic, for example, we examine food chains as required by the National Curriculum for Science. The way that human intervention in food chains can lead to a build up of toxic materials (on the pyramid principle) is not addressed until Key Stage 3, but there is no reason why younger children should not be made aware of this factor. Similarly, the Science curriculum states that children should learn "that plant growth is affected by the availability of light and water and by temperature". Is there any reason why teachers should not also add pollution, pesticides and fertilisers as further variables or ask what factors might affect the availability of sufficient light, water, and temperature? After all, the National Curriculum is stating the minimum, not the only requirements.

Environmental Education in non-topic work. The choice of resource material can make a big difference to the quality of routine practice tasks in the classroom. The skills and attitudes identified in *Curriculum Guidance 7* can be encouraged at all times by making them part of your planning. In English, for example, stories and poems on environmental themes can be read or used for other textual work. Maths work on data and statistics arises naturally from many environmental investigations. Discussing and designing environmentally-friendly play equipment or vehicles can lead on to discussing what real needs are served by many of our technological 'improvements', especially when choice of materials and disposability are taken into account. Looking at the traditions, beliefs, myths and attitudes to Earth and nature of different cultures can form part of RE work, while giving children a broader and more tolerant view of the world at the same time.

ORGANISATIONAL STRATEGIES

While the focus is still on what happens in the classroom, we need to consider the choice of teaching methods. The news media often divides education into 'formal' or 'traditional' and 'progressive'. In reality education is much more subtle than this, and observers have often been misled. When children are allowed to walk around the room, is this a sign of 'informality' or not? When a teacher talks to the whole class at once, does this make her a 'traditional' teacher or merely show she is making a sensible use of her time?

The OFSTED report on Curriculum Organisation and Classroom Practice contains a useful list of factors associated with better classroom practice:

"Carefully planned and appropriate groupings of pupils for tasks.

A mixture of individual, group and whole class teaching.

A manageable number of teaching groups and learning activities, usually four or fewer, provided at any one time.

Carefully planned use of the teacher's time for giving instructions, teaching the whole class, individuals and groups, and moving between activities to instruct, question, explain and assess.

Planned use of the pupils' time including the setting of realistic deadlines for the completion of work.

Clearly established classroom routines and systems."

CURRICULUM ORGANISATION AND CLASSROOM PRACTICE IN PRIMARY SCHOOLS

Environmental Education necessitates consideration of questions of value, attitudes and beliefs. As decisions and solutions are often complex, children need to be given the experience of considering different perspectives, and coming to terms with conflicting points of view. There is a danger that introducing such thorny and paradoxical material to primary children could either overwhelm them or leave them mystified. We should keep the focus of our teaching on action, first-hand experiences, actual case studies, role play games, narrative and fun. This is especially important at Key Stage 1, but even Key Stage 2 children have a limited appetite for the purely theoretical. In this way, children will be prepared for the responses they will have to make to a range of problems throughout their lives.

So a good rule to remember when planning for Environmental Education is 'keep it practical'. Whenever you find yourself writing the word 'discussion' in your session plans, see if a more practical activity could be more effective, followed if necessary by some discussion time. Suggestions include: look at, touch, explain, think about, work out, sort, compare, make a plan, act out, design, find out, consult, share, choose between, play a game. Many of these activities require the teacher to prepare materials in advance, whereas a 'discussion' can be held with no resource material at all. And many also require the children to work autonomously and co-operatively in groups, rather than work as a class with the teacher leading the discussion. You have to consider honestly which strategy will give the most valuable learning opportunities.

The school week does not contain many hours (although it may sometimes feel endless), and a child's school life is soon over. At any time of day teachers should be able to justify to an imaginary inspector why they have asked the children to do whatever they are doing, and what the learning benefits are intended to be. There is plenty of guidance in the National Curriculum subject documents on attitudes, skills and knowledge, so the following paragraphs are merely to focus your thoughts towards education for sustainability.

ATTITUDES

The five attitudes identified in *Curriculum Guidance 7* give a brief overview of how the Government hopes that Environmental Education will affect the values of young people. In *The School is Us*, a WWF book, there is a fuller list of attitudes that may help you as you plan your teaching. A commitment to global equality will not be fostered if you habitually treat boys and girls differently. We cannot expect children to develop a sense of self worth if we do not praise them and listen to their opinions.

What can sustainability bring.

"**Concern for justice:** valuing genuinely democratic principles and processes at all levels and being ready to work for a more just world. — *There throughout*

Rights and responsibilities: A commitment to defending their own rights and the rights of others, and linked to that a commitment to carrying out responsibilities. — *nice environment, responsible for keep their things*

Commitment to equality: A commitment to the principle of equality as the basis on which relationships between individuals, groups and societies should be organised.

Empathy: An openness to imagining the feelings and viewpoints of other people, particularly people in cultures and situations different from their own.

Active participation: A belief that people can usu...   ...n, and that it is usually more effective to take the initi...   ...thers or wait for things to happen

...their own particular
...th new situations

...a recognition of

...of interest and

...e of responsibility

THE SCHOOL IS US

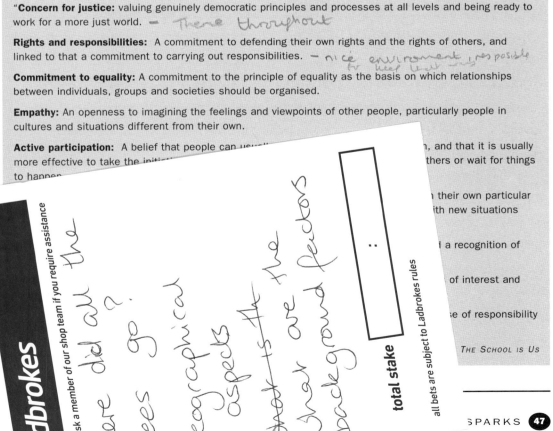

Ladbrokes

please ask a member of our shop team if you require assistance

Where did all the Bees go.

Geographical aspects

What is the What are the background factors

total stake

all bets are subject to Ladbrokes rules

A thread which runs through all of these is that of action: *"...ready to work for a more just world...", "... a commitment to carrying out responsibilities...", "...to take the initiative... "*. If we really wish children to grow up willing and able to change the world, and that is what education for sustainability must mean, then we have to show them from an early age that their actions can have some effect. On your teaching practices you may not have much opportunity to involve children in genuine action for the environment, but once you have a permanent post you can seek ways to involve children in real local issues. These could be as local as helping to redesign the layout of the classroom, or as wide as presenting proposals to the local council to make cycling in the town safer.

KNOWLEDGE

It is very tempting to want to give children as much information as possible about environmental issues. However, we must remember that knowledge on its own is of very little value without understanding. You may know that H_2O is water, but what does this mean? Understanding is vital to knowledge, and is developmental. This means that although you can teach facts to children of any age, the understanding or concepts behind the facts will not be accessible to them until they have reached the appropriate cognitive level in their development. Knowledge about environmental issues is much more a question of concepts and principles than it is of facts. As you plan your teaching, keep in mind the importance of understanding and then you will not offer children knowledge that they have no means of using. The knowledge component of Environmental Education in the National Curriculum is more or less limited to knowledge of natural systems, science and technology, and human effects on the environment. However, children also need to be introduced to knowledge about the social, economic, political and ideological systems which underly our relationship with the environment. This may seem very high flown for primary-age children, but much can be done through stories, case studies, role play and explorations of the children's own attitudes: *"Why is it so important for some children that they have ... trainers?"* Many activities in materials from organisations like Oxfam can help children learn about trading systems, for example, and issues of fairness and justice on a local and global scale.

SKILLS

Skills which are transferable across many areas of thought are known as cross-curricular skills and are very much the backbone of primary teaching. They have already been quoted to illustrate the way in which *Curriculum Guidance 7* can be implemented (see pages 42 and 43).

One of those skills which is particularly relevant to environmental education is "working co-operatively with others". Teamwork and the pooling of ideas will always be vital in finding solutions to both local and global problems; in fact, working co-operatively, respecting others' rights and viewpoints, could prevent many problems arising. In addition, learning to co-operate at an early age is a vital component of education for sustainability as it gives children the opportunity to:

"...gain concrete experience of the highly complex concept of interdependence. This notion will be essential to later studies of relationships between ethnic groups and countries, of ecosystems, of world economics and of public health, to name but a few areas of applicability."

EARTHRIGHTS: EDUCATION AS IF THE PLANET REALLY MATTERED

One skill which does not specifically appear in the *Curriculum Guidance 7* list is that of socially critical thinking, although it could be considered as part of study and problem-solving skills. For example, identifying the cause of air pollution in the town centre as 'too many cars' is only a start. Even quite young children can go on to question why there are so many; what measures would help people to use their cars less; how people are persuaded they need a car; who really benefits... Primary-age children are quite capable of analysing car advertisements and may well be experts in television commercials.

Remember, if our skills are to be really useful to us then we need plenty of practice. It is quite helpful to think of the primary curriculum as a spiral. As children pass through the school they work with the same skills again and again, developing more fluency as they get older, and working with different subject material. *Sustainability is hidden curriculum and occurs throughout it and*

GLOBAL CONNECTIONS

Although most of the children's investigations will probably be into local issues, they also need to be introduced to the wider picture. It is now a commonplace that we live in an increasingly global society: our lives are linked wth others throughout the world, sometimes as equal partners, but frequently in a very inequitable relationship. In particular, our Western affluent lifestyles directly and indirectly have a negative impact on the lives and environments of many people of the South. Even primary children can begin to explore these links.

"Exploring, discussing and understanding these historical, geographical, economic, political and social links is a vital part of every child's education and preparation for being a citizen of the world in the 21st century. In this technological world of rapid communication, children are ready to investigate, discuss and understand the complexities of the world in which we all live."

GLOBAL PERSPECTIVES IN THE NATIONAL CURRICULUM: GUIDANCE FOR KEY STAGES 1 AND 2

Case studies of real trade links, of real people and their lives can help foster a sense of identification and solidarity. Connections can be made in other ways too. A local fight to save old trees from the motorway bulldozers can be linked with the people of the Amazon and the Chipko movement in India, where the idea orginated of hugging trees to save them from the axe.

FUTURES

An important part of Environmental Education is to get children to think about the kind of future they would like. From this rather unfocused start, we can move the children towards thinking about what steps need to be taken and what attitudes need to change to make their futures a reality. They need to understand that the future is not something that just happens, and that they do have power to do something about it. Illustrations can be given about successful initiatives, about other cultures, traditional and modern, where different social and governmental systems operate. Some activities can be based on the short-term, immediate and preferably realisable future, for example, what kind of playground would they like? Moving to a more remote future, and asking what kind of house they might like in the future, may lead to a 'technofix' attitude, where ideas from computer games and films swamp any others. Encourage children to think more deeply about the issues and consider some of the social and environmental effects of the innovations they are predicting.

Much environmental work can be given a more positive slant by starting with the 'preferred future' angle. Rather than starting with *"Our street is dirty and ugly; they ought to ..."*, we could start with *"We would like a clean street with lots of trees and not too much traffic. What steps need to be taken to achieve this?"* By stating the problem in this way, we encourage the idea of 'empowerment', and show the children that they have both the right and the responsibility to make choices. If there are things we cannot make choices about, like Government policies and spending, then we have democratic power to make our voices heard through the ballot box, through letter-writing, joining political parties, pressure groups, lobbying and protesting. It is not a teacher's job to be too political in this, but neither is it subversive in any way to inform the children of these rights and responsibilities and to give them practice in them from an early age.

local authority

APPRECIATION

Finally, we must not forget that an important part of Environmental Education is to celebrate the joy of living in this beautiful world. We would do children a great disservice if we dwelt only on the problems and tragedies. We can help them to develop an appreciation of good architecture, of well designed public open spaces, of lovingly cared for gardens and window boxes and, of course, for the natural world. Although considered by some modern critics as not really being what Environmental Education is about, in our opinion it is important for children to have contact with good old-fashioned nature. In a 1994 BBC radio programme, a speaker reported that a group of new nursery children, when presented with brightly coloured wheely toys and other equipment, rushed instead to a small patch of grass where they *"hurled themselves on it, rolling on it, smelling it, clutching it"* and refused to leave it.

Pond-dipping and planting buddleia bushes to attract butterflies may not be radical, but they do bring children into direct contact with the world we are trying to save. Children who do not believe – as reported on the same radio programme – that apples grow on trees, but come ready made in supermarket boxes, are not likely to have an interest in investigating the pros and cons of pesticide use.

And my heart soars

The beauty of the trees,
the softness of the air,
the fragrance of the grass,
    speak to me.

The summit of the mountain,
The thunder of the sky,
the rhythm of the sea,
    speak to me.

The faintness of the stars,
the freshness of the morning,
the dewdrop of the flower,
    speak to me.

The strength of fire,
the taste of salmon,
the trail of the sun,
and the life that never goes away,
    They speak to me.

And my heart soars.

CHIEF DAN GEORGE

References

ENVIRONMENTAL EDUCATION:
A FRAMEWORK FOR THE DEVELOPMENT
OF A CROSS-CURRICULAR THEME IN
WALES, *Advisory Paper 17, CCW, 1992*

CURRICULUM GUIDANCE 7:
ENVIRONMENTAL EDUCATION
NCC, HMSO, 1990

THE NATIONAL CURRICULUM AND ITS
ASSESSMENT
Sir Ron Dearing, SCAA, 1994

TEACHING ENVIRONMENTAL MATTERS
THROUGH THE NATIONAL CURRICULUM
SCAA, 1996

GOVERNMENT STRATEGY FOR
ENVIRONMENTAL EDUCATION IN ENGLAND
DfEE, DOE, 1997

COMPETENCIES OF THE ENVIRONMENTALLY
EDUCATED TEACHER
UNESCO-UNEP, 1990

THE TREATMENT OF POLITICALLY
CONTROVERSIAL ISSUES IN SCHOOLS
Draft Circular on The Education (No 2) Act 1986, DES

MAKING GLOBAL CONNECTIONS
*David Hicks and Miriam Steiner (EDS.), Oliver & Boyd,
1989*

PLANNING AND EVALUATION OF
ENVIRONMENTAL EDUCATION
*Christiane Dorion,
WWF-UK/CEE/The University of Reading, 1993*

CURRICULUM ORGANISATION AND
CLASSROOM PRACTICE IN PRIMARY
SCHOOLS: A FOLLOW UP REPORT
OFSTED, DFEE, 1993

THE SCHOOL IS US
Linnea Renton, WWF-UK/Manchester DEP, 1993

COSTING THE EARTH
BBC Radio 4, Autumn 1994

EARTHRIGHTS: EDUCATION AS IF THE
PLANET REALLY MATTERED
Greig, Pike and Selby, WWF-UK/Kogan Page, 1987

GLOBAL PERSPECTIVES IN THE NATIONAL
CURRICULUM: GUIDANCE FOR KEY
STAGES 1 AND 2
Kathy Midwinter (ED), DEA, 1995

THREE TOPICS

In the next three chapters, there is a detailed look at three topics that are commonly taught in primary schools, 'My home, my street', 'Journeys' and 'Food'. Each has been written for a different age-group (Years 1/2, Year 4 and Year 6), and each shows how Environmental Education can be introduced.

Each chapter is arranged the same way. First there is some background information, both about how the topic might be taught and also about the environmental issues. This is written at your level, and is to help you become more knowledgeable about the subject. If you had to plan another topic in the same way, you would need to do what the writers have done here, and research available books and packages of materials. The better informed you are, the more confident you will be and the more enjoyable your teaching will be. However good the resources of a school, the best resource in every classroom is the teacher.

Next there is a topic in outline, together with some planning considerations and expected outcomes. This is done in the form of a brief a student might be given by a school when going to do school experience. The staff will have worked out roughly how the topic might be organised, bearing in mind the knowledge, skills and attitudes that should be covered to satisfy the National Curriculum. There is more content here than is required by the National Curriculum Orders, but it would be fitted into the extra 20% of time schools should have to use at their discretion. Some of the 'expected outcomes' have been stipulated by the school planners, others have been the ideas of our own hypothetical student.

In years 1 and 2, topic work often covers wide areas of the curriculum, as does our 'My home, my street', but there are specific targets for each of the four or five subjects. 'Journeys' concentrates on just two subjects, and 'Food' on just one. All these types of organisation are common.

You as a student, or later as a teacher, would have the chance to work on this topic outline in any way you chose, and this is what is shown in the third section. We show some key excerpts from the plan as it might have been worked on by a student or teacher, chosen to illustrate how Environmental Education is integrated into the topic. Other activities are mentioned briefly to show how the student has covered other National Curriculum requirements, but even within these there might well be an environmental component.

PART 6

As you look at the plan, notice that the suggested study areas are not given as actual sessions. Some of the activities could be put together and all done during one session. For example, a talk from you (giving information), some research in reference books, and some written notes are three activities that naturally form a complete session. Other activities could be done simultaneously by different groups. This is a useful way of working when resources are scarce: one group could be doing an experiment, another drawing maps, another painting and another looking at photographs and making notes. Yet again, some activities in the outline plan may take a lot longer to complete, so they would become all, or part, of several sessions.

Bear in mind also that this is still only a skeleton plan. As well as the suggested activities, stories, displays, word lists, book collections and general talk with the children will all contribute to the overall learning of the topic.

The fourth section in each topic shows actual session plans, two each for 'My home, my street' and 'Journeys', and one for 'Food'. We hope that as you read through them you will see the session unfolding in your mind's eye. Although they are written to a consistent format, we have not used the kind of printed form you may have been used to. In our experience, students need more space to expand their teaching ideas, and different sections will need more or less space depending on what type of session they are. In the 'Food' topic, instead of a second session plan, there is guidance on planning a visit. Environmental education often involves a day or half day trip, and the advice can easily be adapted for any destination.

It may seem pedantic to write out the questions you are going to ask the children. However, by writing them down you rehearse the session in your head, and this gives you confidence when you are in front of the class. It is so easy in the heat of the moment, when you are concentrating on organising children and resources, for your planned teaching points to fly out of your head.

As the session plans are hypothetical, we have left the 'evaluation' sections blank, but it is an essential part of any real teaching session. We have already stressed the importance of critical reflection in improving your teaching effectiveness (see Part 5). When writing an evaluation, try to make your comments as specific as possible; for example, *"It went quite well and the children worked quite hard"* is not nearly as useful as *"I hurried over the discussion because I was worried about the time, so only the top group really understood what they had to do and I had to explain to individuals all through the rest of the session. Next time I will question the children after the discussion because it will save time in the end."* As well as thinking about the content of a session, make notes on your strategies: *"I didn't allow the children enough genuine choice about how to go forward,"* and notes for the future: *"I need to make sure Daniel receives some confidence boosting,"* or *"The Red Group need help in working co-operatively."*

The next section of each topic is headed 'Over to you'. As in earlier chapters, this is an invitation to look behind the suggestions here and to think of ideas yourself. The main purpose of this book is to show you how to tackle a topic from an Environmental Education angle. We hope you will be able to apply a similar planning process to any topic you have to teach.

Lastly, there is a resources section for each topic. A few fiction and reference books have been listed but obviously there are many, many more. Useful addresses are also included. Some of these could prove equally useful for other topic areas as well. You will find that firms and charities are very generous with their materials, which often include information sheets, videos and packs especially written for primary schools. It is important that you evaluate these critically before using them and make sure that not only are they suitable for the age and experience of your children and the curriculum requirements you are planning, but that the hidden messages they are conveying are also those you wish to encourage or that you can explicitly discuss with the children.

MY HOME, MY STREET

A Topic for Key Stage 1, Years 1 and 2

At Key Stage 1 topics are often chosen which relate directly to the children's own experience and 'Homes' is an obvious choice. Here it has been widened to include a child's own street (which may be some way from the school) to introduce the idea of the child as part of a community, and some study of the area around the school is undertaken. The children are also introduced to homes in other countries and how they reflect local conditions. The class consists of both Year 1 and Year 2 pupils and the teacher would have to take this into account when planning the work.

CORE AND FOUNDATION SUBJECTS

As often happens at Key Stage 1, large areas of the curriculum are covered during the six weeks of this topic, but main curriculum focuses are Geography, Science, History, Technology and English, with a little History. The Maths syllabus runs separately, although some activities would be linked into the topic wherever possible. A teacher might well also link in Music with songs about homes, for example.

Because this project is covering so many curriculum areas, the time allocated to it throughout the week is quite high. All the children's Science, Geography and Technology for this six weeks is included as part of the topic, and much of their English work. Although sessions may be timetabled, the school day for Key Stage 1 is often fairly flexible.

ENVIRONMENTAL EDUCATION

As you will see from the outline plan, the school in this case has specified that Environmental Education must have a place in this topic. A few activities that our student designs can definitely be considered 'environmental', but also, if you look at all the activities, you will see that some of the goals of Environmental Education could be planned for through the teaching and learning styles, and the encouragement of attitudes and values.

Not all of the issues mentioned below would be covered in a single six-week topic and not all would be suitable anyway for Key Stage 1. For example, children need a basic understanding of how we depend on electricity in the home before they are introduced to ideas of energy production, its environmental consequences, and ways of saving energy. But as children consider their own homes, they can be introduced to some of the world's diversity of homes, and as they do this, issues of supply and demand, needs and wants, fairness and unfairness, and living sustainably will naturally arise.

The issues

HOME IS WHERE THE HEART IS

For most people, and certainly most children, their home is of central importance in their lives. It may be a semi-detached bungalow, a traveller's bus, a children's home, a one-roomed adobe hut or a nomad's tent, but it is where the child begins to discover and affirm their own identity, through interaction with other people and the local environment. It is, ideally, where they feel safe and where they begin to explore relationships and ideas of rights and responsibilities.

"Now, with a rush of old memories, how clearly it stood up before him, in the darkness! Shabby indeed, and small and poorly furnished, and yet his, the home he had made for himself, the home he had been so happy to get back to after his day's work..."
The Mole related "how this was planned, how that was thought out, and how this was got through a windfall from an aunt, and that was a wonderful bargain, and this other thing was bought out of laborious savings and a certain amount of 'going without'."

KENNETH GRAHAME,
THE WIND IN THE WILLOWS

The home is the environment that people usually care about most and where they learn to care – or not care – about their surroundings in general. In a row of identical houses the residents will nearly always make changes or additions to the outside and decorate the inside to their own taste. Students in anonymous bedsits and prisoners in cells are equally likely to cover the walls with posters. Children, too, like to have their own space, even it is only a corner of a bedroom. When they are able to, people change their homes to suit their changing circumstances – knocking down walls, changing bedrooms to bathrooms or darkrooms, building patios and granny annexes... (This can cause problems in the community – should people have a free hand to do as they wish with their houses, even if their neighbours, or the local planning authority, think it spoils the general look of a neighbourhood?)

Because the home environment is so important, those who have responsibility for planning housing have a critical role. We need, at the very least, to be comfortable with where we live. Back-to-back coal-mining towns of the Victorian era and city tower block estates of the 1960s were both built with economics and practical considerations as the guiding principles – how to get a lot of people into a small space for minimum cost. Nowadays it seems that more thought is being given to making new housing more 'people-friendly' even where space is limited, and

"A woman has come up with a novel approach to the housing problem: she has made a home in the stairwell of Brixton Registry Office. The unidentified woman had put up curtains and hung paintings on the wall. 'She has made it really homely down there', a Registry Office worker said."

THE BIG ISSUE,
OCTOBER/NOVEMBER, 1994

there are encouraging initiatives where local authority architects work with the future residents when planning a new estate.

We rightly see as one of the greatest ills of our time the huge numbers of homeless people. It is especially distressing when we hear of the plight of the thousands of 'street children', often harassed by the police, who fend entirely for themselves in some of the cities in the poorer world. But in our own society there are far too many families in bed and breakfast accommodation who have no place to call home and there are thousands of people sleeping rough on our city streets. Many of them opt for the limited sense of security and familiarity of returning to the same place each night, even if it is only to the same shop doorway. The authorities both here and in other countries see the temporary shelters under the railway arches and the burgeoning shanty towns on the edge of the big cities as 'a problem' but, in reality, they are a resourceful *answer* to a problem.

"ACTING LOCAL"

What these people are doing is what people have always done – building homes from locally available materials. In the Cotswolds it was limestone blocks; in London, bricks baked from local clay; in Amazonia, palm fronds; in Sweden, timber; in North Africa, tents made from animal hide. People have always shown remarkable ingenuity in using whatever is to hand and which suits the climate and way of life. In Britain, for example, the traditional pitched roof is a defence against rain and snow; and the solidly built houses suit a settled people who lived in one place for generation after generation. In the Malaysian rainforest, by contrast, houses are built which are deliberately made not to last; the people move on every few years when the land has become overused and the game has moved away. The houses fall down and rot, recycling the nutrients and eventually returning the forest to itself.

DUST TO DUST

Houses like that are perhaps the ultimate in 'environment-friendly' buildings. They return eventually to a natural state, leaving no trace either of where the materials came from or where the house was. The same is not true for most housing, in whatever part of the world. Stone, slate, clay (for bricks, tiles and cement), chalk or limestone (for cement), sand and gravel (for concrete) are all quarried, often leaving huge unsightly holes. Decisions have to be made about what to do with these: some are filled with water to the advantage of wildlife and windsurfers; others become landfill sites for waste, including building rubble from demolished buildings. These might then be landscaped or built on. (Breeze blocks, interestingly, are made from waste products from coal-fired power stations.)

Unfortunately, when homes in this country are no longer required for some reason, very little usually gets recycled. Stone may be used again but it is often not worth while in time or money terms for a contractor to strip out all the reusable wood or glass or to carefully separate bricks. If things have aesthetic value there is more hope, and items like fireplaces or balustrades are often saved for resale (or removed from builders' skips at dead of night!). Large blocks of flats are usually demolished wholesale and reduced literally to rubble, which then has to be disposed of.

NEEDS AND WANTS

Most people require more from a home than four walls, a roof and the love of the people in it. All human beings have basic needs beyond shelter – warmth (which in some climates is provided sufficiently by the sun), water and food. These we cannot do without and Antarctic explorers, astronauts and seafarers have to take theirs with them. We also need to be able to dispose of wastes in a way that won't contaminate our living space, water or food supply. Further than this, our list of 'needs' merges into one of 'wants'. What we consider essential at home we can well do without on a boating trip or a peace camp; and something *we* consider essential might seem pure luxury to someone who doesn't have it. Our consumer society leads us to think of more and more goods and services as necessities and we need to think carefully about whether a new three-piece suite or the latest technological advance is really doing anything to enhance our quality of life, or whether we are being gulled into needless expense and unnecessary consumption of yet more non-renewable resources and production of yet more waste.

"A blasted power cut, just as I was cleaning my teeth"

LET THERE BE LIGHT (AND HEAT AND POWER)

Energy in the form of electricity and gas are now considered essentials in our society. Our use of energy in the home is one obvious area where we could all make an effort towards living more sustainably. There are many reasons. Most of our power stations are still run on fossil fuels which are non-renewable so will eventually run out (oil and gas possibly within the next 50 years). There is unfair distribution; including fuel for vehicles, the developed countries use 40 times as much fossil fuel as the poorer countries. These power stations pollute the atmosphere, causing acid rain and contributing to global warming. According to Friends of the Earth, if every household in the UK replaced one light bulb with an energy-efficient one, there would be no need for the Sizewell B power station. Nuclear power carries the risk of severe radiation, however tightly controlled it is; wind farms are noisy; hydroelectric dams flood valleys and silt up rivers; tidal barrages bring disruption to wildlife. There is no form of electricity production which does not cause some harm to the environment although solar power is beginning to look promising.

"WATER, WATER EVERYWHERE, NOR YET A DROP (FIT TO) DRINK"

Water supply and sewage disposal are two other vital services, usually firmly linked. The one has to be brought, clean, to where people want it, and the human and water waste has to be disposed of safely. In Britain, the sewage sometimes leads indirectly back into the water supply, requiring expensive cleaning and chemical additives. In some poorer countries, water contaminated by sewage is one of biggest causes of disease and child mortality. Many other contaminants can get into our water supply: run-off from fertilisers and effluent from farms, chemicals and metals from factories, drugs and hormones from the sewers and assorted poisons from landfill rubbish sites. Solid wastes, such as sanitary ware, disposable nappy liners and condoms end up in the sea.

Overall lack of water is also a problem in many parts of the world, in some cases because of scarce rainfall, but also because of over-demand, poor management and leaking pipes. Water tables are dropping, rivers are drying up and aquifers disappearing.

Outline Topic Plan

Duration 6 Weeks

Years 1/2

Topic My Home, My Street

National Curriculum Subjects: English, Maths, Science, Geography, History and Technology

Cross Curricular Themes: Environmental Education, Health Education

School Resources Available: Building Materials, construction sets, camera, reference books, fiction

Details of Subject Areas:

English ATs 1, 2 & 3
Opportunities for discussion, drama/role-play, interviewing someone from local community, using a tape recorder, writing letters, prose and poetry, reading and being read to, learning to write own addresses.

Maths AT 1, 2, 3, 4
Opportunities for looking at shape and number; recording on bar and other charts.

Science AT 1, 2, 3, 4
Humans need food and water; exploring using various senses; sorting and naming building materials; relating understanding of science to domestic and environmental contexts; understanding that many everyday appliances use electricity; constructing and working with simple circuits.

Geography AT 1
Using maps at a variety of scales; investigating quality of children's own immediate environment; studying housing in the area around the school; following a route on a large-scale map; understanding of services that are provided to community; awareness of the world outside their own locality; observing; communicating; recording.

History AT 1
Developing a sense of chronology; awareness of the past and how it was different from the present; changes in the lives of their families and other adults; awareness of how to find out about the past (photographs and memories); reasons and results of changes.

Technology AT 1, 2
Designing and making use of reclaimed materials.

Cross-Curricular Themes:

Environmental Education
Promoting positive attitudes to environment; how humans live in communities; first-hand experiences; use of real-life issues; co-operative learning; variety of approaches to teaching and learning.

Health Education
Safety and health at home.

Planning Considerations:

1. Some of the routine English teaching will be separately planned (handwriting, spelling, phonic practice, reading support).

2. Much of the Maths syllabus will be separately planned.

3. Group activities can be integrated into the day after initial explanation to the class.

Expected Outcomes:

Large local map with children's houses (models) on it.

Class book of writing (accounts and poems).

Letter writing corner set up with materials and display.

Tape-recorded interview to listen to.

Home corner with emphasis on household appliances.

Models of house interiors using construction sets.

Completed electrical circuits with buzzers and lights.

<u>SIX WEEKS TOPIC PLAN</u>

My Home, My Street

<u>Week 1</u>

Activity	Purpose	Notes	Advance Planning
Making a home game	Actively exploring issues of human survival; needs and wants; what is a home? Learning to make co-operative decisions.	Introduce world contexts, does everyone have same needs? How are they met? Emphasise co-operation and validating of opinions.	Make cards.
Rebuilding Bluefields	Understanding lives in a distant environment (Nicaragua); different kinds of houses. The benefits of co-operation. Learning to express empathy through drama.	Tell story of the hurricane in 1988 from 'World Active'. Teach 'in-role' to encourage children to mime the rebuilding or to make up own dialogue.	Prepare outline for dramatising; practise storytelling techniques.
Happy times at home	To encourage positive feelings about home; to convey in writing some of the discussed ideas about homes; to extend vocabulary; to engage with story books.	Encourage children to verbalise their feelings of safety and love. Read some stories that show home situations, including moving house.	Choose story books; prepare useful vocabulary for writing support. Prepare outline for dramatising; practise storytelling techniques

OTHER ACTIVITIES:

Differences between home and school; people who live in my home; different types of home – sorting by different criteria; model from reclaimed materials or drawing or painting of own house or favourite room; poem 'The Old Sailor' by AA Milne.

SIX WEEKS TOPIC PLAN

My Home, My Street

Week 2

Activity	Purpose	Notes	Advance Planning
House building materials and where they come from	Learning about properties of house building materials: considering differences between finite and non-finite resources; environmental effects of raw material extraction	Main emphasis on fun and sorting, but make sure environmental factors are understood.	Collect building materials. Select photos from "Doorways"
From my window I See...	To move children's focus from their own home to the community and local environment. To produce complete piece of writing in poetic form.	Talk about what children see or would like to see from their windows and collect useful words to help their writing. Individual writing can be done on paper with an opening casement printed on it (use photocopier)	Design and copy window format.
Graph of types of homes children live in	Visual record of data collection; understanding that there are different kinds of homes.	Class activity with individual contributions. Ask children to 'read' from completed graph to check that they understand the concept. Compare results with parallel class if possible. See if children can think of reasons for results (for example, not many flats). Information could be entered in computer database.	Choose type of graph and symbols that will be used.

OTHER ACTIVITIES:

Speech bubbles to complete 'Home is ...'; locating home on large-scale map of the area; writing addresses; what is your home made of? properties and uses of house-building materials; playing in the 'Home Corner'; collecting magazine and newspaper pictures of homes; discussing advantages; disadvantages; aesthetics; houses in the past.

SIX WEEKS TOPIC PLAN

My Home, My Street

Week 3

Activity	Purpose	Notes	Advance Planning
Household appliances that use electricity	To understand the importance of electricity in modern life. To consider how jobs would be done without electricity, for example in the past, or in parts of other countries. To think of the future. To consider safety when using electrical appliances.	Group work: children draw appliances carefully from observation. They then present their drawing to the class, explaining the purpose of the power (heat, light, movement), safety aspects and alternative ways of doing the same job. Discuss advantages and disadvantages of electric versus alternative; discuss energy-saving where appropriate.	Bring small appliances to school for a few days (hair dryer, food blender, clock, radio, table lamp, etc.).
My possessions	To consider the differences between 'needs' and 'wants'.	Children draw (and label if they can) all their possessions on small cards. They sort into two piles, or post into two boxes labelled 'Things I Need' and 'Things I Want (or Like'). Further development could be to consider which things need electricity to work or to maintain them (football kit needs washing machine). Keep discussion general, not referring to any one child's cards.	None.
Looking after my home	Understanding that the home environment needs to be cared for, appreciation of the work necessary and how it can be shared.	Children take turns to mime actions for others to guess – housework, repairs, car cleaning, gardening, pet care, etc. Discuss how they can help keep home attractive.	None

OTHER ACTIVITIES:

Small drawing of own house stuck on large scale map of area; finding routes from home to school. Looking at homes near the school and classifying by type. Identifying and drawing shapes in the buildings. Other activities from *Doorways*.

SIX WEEKS TOPIC PLAN

My Home, My Street

Week 4

Activity	Purpose	Notes	Advance Planning
Compare photos of homes around the world	Observing and communicating. Using new vocabulary. Teaching the diversity of dwellings and their fitness for their purpose and local environment.	Use photos from 'Doorways'. Children work in pairs and one describes photo without the other seeing it. Second child tries to draw what is being described. General discussion of what can be inferred about local environment from type of dwelling. Make sure to include city photos from the South.	Sort out appropriate photos from pack.
Housing in Kenya	Learning about a location that contrasts with the local one. Hearing about a positive example of people (especially women) taking responsibility for local improvements.	Use Intermediate Technology materials on Maasai housing but tell as a story rather than an account. Emphasise that the women took the initiative to improve their smoky houses. Children respond to story in some way (art, drama, writing).	None.
Comparing lifestyles in Kenya and UK	To reinforce knowledge and empathy for another culture. To compare energy use in developed and developing countries. To appreciate universality of human needs.	Use photographs from "Feeling good about faraway friends" Be aware of stereotyping – ie electricity is widely used in the developing world.	Sort out appropriate photos from pack.

OTHER ACTIVITIES:

Further activities from pack. Making circular structures with roofs modelled on Maasai houses. Testing flat and conical roofs for strength. Recording findings. Continuing to explore shapes in buildings, looking at roofs and chimneys. Preparing questions to ask postal worker next week.

SIX WEEKS TOPIC PLAN

My Home, My Street

Week 5

Activity	Purpose	Notes	Advance Planning
Imaginary Walk	Children remember their own street; retell and draw or paint their mental pictures.	Teacher-led guided visualisation to help children recall landmarks around their homes. Encourage opinion and feelings; 'Is it noisy or quiet? Is it raining or sunny? How do you feel?'	None.
Likes and dislikes of my street	To encourage children to be pro-active and feel responsible towards their own environment; to help them formulate their opinions.	Use 'Smiley' and 'Grumpy' face categories to collect lists from the children of likes and dislikes. Those who live in the same street could work together. Discuss ways in which street environment could be changed for the better.	None.
Interview with Postman	To show how one service reaches each house; to practise speaking and listening for a particular purpose; to bring a member of the community into the classroom.	Use pre-planned questions and tape record the interview. Let children show visitor the work and displays connected with the topic.	Write to local Sorting Office to find someone willing to come; prepare questions with children; get tape recorder ready.

OTHER ACTIVITIES:

Moving house discussed using some relevant stories. Family memories discussed. Writing based on the 'Smiley' face work. Street numbers – counting in twos, odds and evens.

Class 'thank you' letter to guest. Constructing and working with simple electrical circuits, show how doorbell works.

SIX WEEKS TOPIC PLAN

My Home, My Street

Week 6

Activity	Purpose	Notes	Advance Planning
How services get to my house	To show children that gas, electricity, water and sewage are connected to houses. To encourage them to ask 'how?'.	Discuss basic ideas then walk round the outside of the school noting drains, electricity cables and so on. Children may suggest that some services are delivered underground. Ask them to find out about their homes and report back next day.	None.
Where does electricity come from?	To find out what children already know. To introduce the idea that electricity has to be 'produced' in some way and that there is always an environmental cost.	Brainstorm and list ideas, add basic information where necessary. Show photos of power station, wind farm, dam. Elicit ideas of environmental harm. Brief and simple discussion, stressing local effects.	Find photos.
The house I would like to live in in the future	To encourage invention and speculation; to think about energy efficiency; writing in continuous prose.	Refer back to energy discussion. Writing support given to children with vocabulary displayed and scribing if necessary. Labelled drawings can also be used.	None.

OTHER ACTIVITIES:

Painting of houses of the future; uses of water in the home; rubbings of pavement covers for gas, electricity, water, service points; photograph quiz of street objects – what is their purpose?

Week One

Activity Title: Making a Home Game

Date: 7th January...   **Time:** 1.00 pm   **Duration:** 1 hour.

Group: Class   **Age:** Year 1/2   **Place:** Classroom

Curriculum Focus:
Mainly introduction, but also Science: survival needs of humans.

Preparation and Resources:
House shaped card for each group with 3x3 grid of spaces to collect 9 cards. Number of groups X 12 small cards. 1 for each group of: water, fire, light, furniture, lavatory, telephone, television, pet, love, food, toys, garden. Word and symbol on each card, blank on back. Music triangle.

Learning Objectives:
1. Children will understand basic requirements for survival.
2. Children will make value judgements about 'wants' as extra to their 'needs'.
3. Children will begin to see that basic requirements are common to all people of the world.
4. Children will exchange their cards by persuasion.
5. Children will work co-operatively, making decisions as a group and swapping between groups.

Activity Outline:
Introduction, group game, discussion.

Organisation of Children and Resources:
Children sit on mat then split into groups. Each group needs a place for collaborative discussion.

Session Structure

1. *Introduction*
Sit class on mat. Show house-shaped card for each group. Explain that they have to fill in the card with little cards to make their group 'home'. Ask how many cards it takes to fill house shape (9), and how many will be left over (3). Ask them to get into 5 groups still on mat.

Show the small cards and explain the symbols, ie fire = warmth and cooking; light = all lights in house. Do not comment on the relative importance of the cards (ie water more important than pet). Check that they are not confused. Explain that they need to go to 'market', swapping cards they do not want for cards they do want. Only one 'messenger' is to go out swapping to the market place (the mat) at any one time, taking only one card. The signal for swapping at the market will be my striking the triangle. A different messenger goes out each time. When group is happy with the selection of cards, a messenger takes the spare cards to the market and leaves them for others to choose. They sit in a line and wait for other groups to finish. There is no 'right' answer; the choice of cards is up to the group.

2. Development

Playing the game, shuffle all the little cards and place them face down. Each group picks up 12 of these and a house-shaped base card and goes to a corner of the room. They lay cards out and discuss which to swap and who will do it. Ring the triangle for first messengers to come to the mat to make swaps. If they cannot find a swapper, they must go back, wait for the next ring and let another messenger try with the same card or another card. Continue until all groups are satisfied or cannot make any more swaps.

3. Conclusion

Bring home cards to the mat. Each group choose a spokesperson to explain their choice of cards and which of the 12 they have decided not to use. Discuss the differences. Listen to comments and complaints. Questions could include:

1. Are you pleased with your home?

2. Did you have a card you would not think of swapping because it was so good? (use 'good' rather than 'useful').

3. Which card did you want to swap straight away? Why?

4. Which cards have you all got? Can you think why?

5. Which would you not have on a camping trip? Which would you miss the most?

6. If you did not have water in the house, what would you do?

7. Can you think of anywhere in the world where people might not have fire?

8. Were there any cards you would have liked which were not in the game? Why?

See if children make a distinction between essential cards (needs) and luxuries (wants). After session, display home cards on a side table for a few days to encourage continuation of discussion.

Evaluation:

Session Plan 2

<u>Week</u>   *Two*

<u>Activity Title:</u>   *House building materials and where they come from*

<u>Date:</u> *12th January*   <u>Time:</u>   *9.10 am*   <u>Duration:</u> *90 minutes*

<u>Group:</u>   *Class and then groups*   <u>Age:</u> *Years 1/2*   <u>Place:</u>   *Classroom*

Curriculum Focus: Science

Preparation and Resources:
Bring in brick, tile, slate, drainpipe, drain cover, electricity circuit, gutter, window frame. Cards with name for each object. Other cards with name of raw materials objects are made from. Curtain or sheet to cover table.
Find pictures and reference books. Prepare art materials.
Select photos from "Doorways" pack

Learning Objectives:

1. Children will identify common building materials and perhaps note their own regional differences. New vocabulary.

2. Children will use senses to explore and sort materials.

3. Children will start to appreciate that materials are chosen for specific uses on the basis of their properties and that a material can have a variety o uses.

4. Children will begin to understand the methods of obtaining raw materials for house-building and realise that factory processes are involved.

5. Children will be introduced to ideas of sustainability of building resources.

6. Children will begin to consider the idea of different buildings suiting different environments.

Activity Outline:
Looking at, touching, naming and discussing building materials.
   Follow up art activities.

Organisation of Children and Resources:
Hide all building materials under a table hidden by a cloth before the children come into the room. Have labels ready. Sit children in a group near the table. Prepare art activities on other tables.

Session Structure

Introduction

Introduce idea of 'What is your house made of?'. Discuss for a few minutes, noticing what children already know and their vocabulary. Collect words on blackboard or large piece of paper as they suggest them.

Send individual children into the 'Builder's Store' (ie under the table) to choose an item and bring it out. Children identify it and place it on floor with label on it. Continue until store is empty.

Development

1. Discuss what each item is made from. Children handle and describe weight, texture, etc. Explain that natural materials (clay, wood, iron, lime) have to go through factory processes to make house component. Teach that glass comes from sand, plastic from oil, both natural resources. Label each item with its raw material. Muddle labels up and see if children can put them back.

2. Where do these materials come from? Show pictures of tree felling, quarrying and mining. Ask if these resources will go on for ever. What will happen to the holes in the ground?

3. Show some photos from "Doorways" and elicit children's ideas about building materials. Discuss where the building materials might have come from. Are they 'natural' or manufactured?

4. Group activities (children choose)

a) One group do observational drawings of building materials.

b) One group draw quarry, brickworks, timber felling (use reference books).

c) One group make crayon rubbings of wood (use floor or plank) and brick (use outside wall). Children cut up these two sheets to make collage picture of their own house, using brick and wood papers appropriately. Could use clear plastic for windows.

d) Group discuss and draw uses for an old quarry.

Conclusion

Leave materials on side table with labels and encourage informal discussions and various sorting activities.

Read Chapter 1 of "The House at Pooh Corner" by A. A. Milne, 'in which a house is built for Eeyore at Pooh Corner'. If appropriate, the first 5 pages can be omitted as the action takes a long time to get going.

Evaluation:

1. Can you think of any alternative visitors who demonstrate the links between the child and the community? How would you prepare to follow-up the visit? For example, a plumber could be asked to come and show/explain tools of the trade, and you could display some tools alongside Mrs Plug the Plumber, by The Ahlbergs ('Happy Families' series).

2. Have a look at some reference books to make sure that they present an accurate and up-to-date picture of the world.

3. Can you think of some sessions that would teach about water in the home?

4. Look through the plans and see if you can identify the teaching styles and class organisation that reflect the aim of Environmental Education as outlined in the diagram on pages 42 and 43.

RESOURCES

Curriculum Materials

WORLD ACTIVE – FACTS AND PUZZLES ABOUT OUR WORLD

by Deborah Manley with OXFAM, Piccolo, 1992.

This is where to find the story of Bluefields, Nicaragua, mentioned in the Week 1 Topic Plan. The people of Bluefields worked co-operatively to rebuild their houses after the hurricane of 1988.

MAASAI HOUSES IN KENYA

The women of Maasai worked with the charity Intermediate Technology to redesign their houses so that smoke from cooking would not be trapped inside the house and cause chest complaints. The story can be obtained from Intermediate Technology, Myson House, Railway Terrace, Rugby, CV21 3HT. Tel: 01788 560631.

DOORWAYS

Save the Children, 1987.

Available from Save the Children Fund, Mary Datchelor House, 17 Grove Lane, London, SE5 8RD; also available from OXFAM.

This pack includes a set of 24 photographs of homes around the world, inside and out, rich and poor. The pack is about global housing issue, homelesness and housing schemes and, although aimed at older children, some of the activities and discussion points could be adapted for years 1 and 2.

FEELING GOOD ABOUT FARAWAY FRIENDS, DAILY LIFE OF A MAASAI FAMILY IN KENYA

Leeds DEC, 1995

This provides pupils with opportunities to explore their feelings about their own localities and also to relate to real people in a distant locality. Excellent colour photos and extensive information for teachers.

HOMES

Scottish Development Education Centre/Save the Children, 1991.

Available from Scottish DEC, Old Playhouse Close, Moray Institute of Education, Holyrood House, Edinburgh, EH8 8AQ, or Save the Children Fund, (address as above); also available from OXFAM.

Using 21 colour photographs and a number of activity sheets, this book focuses on three families – in Scotland, Malaysia and China. It explores ideas about what makes a home, family roles, community and the right to shelter.

NEW FACES, NEW PLACES

Save the Children, 1992.

Available from Save the Children Fund, (address as above)

Real life stories from around the world about people who have left the security and familiarity of their homes to move elsewhere. The stories could be read aloud at story time, or some Year 1 and 2 children would be able to read them alone. There are also ideas for activities and discusion on homes in general.

NEW JOURNEYS

Birmingham Development Education Centre, 1992.

Available from Birmingham DEC, Gillett Centre, 998 Bristol Road, Selly Oak, Birmingham, B29 6LE; also available from OXFAM.

Although aimed at older children and with a different purpose, the photographs of everyday life in Tanzania and Kenya could be valuable in widening young children's perceptions of people in Kenya.

Fiction and Non-fiction Books

FICTION

MR PLUM'S OASIS

Eliza Trimby, Faber, 1981.

Two neighbours in a dingy street work together to create a beautiful garden which spreads and spreads to the greater benefit of people and wildlife alike.

WINDOW

Jeannie Baker, Red Fox Books, 1991.

A wordless book with beautiful collage pictures. The view from the window changes over the years from wild, rich Australian countryside to city streets.

BRINGING THE RAIN TO KAPITI PLAIN

Verna Aardema and Beatriz Vidal, Picturemac, 1986.

Based on a Kenyan folk tale, this tells the story of Ki-pat the herdsman in simple rhyming text. Beautiful illustrations show the animals and people of the Kenyan plain.

MCHESI GOES TO MARKET AND MCHESI GOES TO THE GAME PARK

Jacaranda Designs Ltd, 1992.

Two delightful picture stories with dual-language texts, set in Kenya, which will help to show it as a real place. Imported from Kenya and available from Letterbox Library, Unit 2D, Leroy House, 436 Essex Road, London, N1 3QP.

(To buy these books you need to be a member of this Book Club, but it is well worth it anyway. They specialise in non-sexist and multicultural books for children.)

DON'T FORGET TO WRITE

Martina Selway, Red Fox, 1993.

Excellent story in the form of letters from Rosie to her Mum. Rosie gradually learns not to be homesick and to enjoy her stay with Granny, Granddad and Auntie Mabel.

THE TWIG THING

Jan Mark, Puffin, 1990.

Another moving house book, this time with solo Dad. Written with heart, good for newly independent readers.

KATIE MORAG AND THE TWO GRANDMOTHERS

Mairi Hadderwick, Picture Lion, 1985.

A Hebrides Island story that is in most school libraries. Others in series.

GRANDMA'S BILL

Martin Waddell, Simon and Schuster, 1990.

One of Martin Waddell's best, giving children insights into how the generations of a family are linked by photographs and memories. Very moving.

THE PATCHWORK QUILT

Valerie Flournoy, Puffin, 1985.

Another story celebrating families and grandmothers, this time with an Afro-Caribbean background.

ALEX'S BED,

Mary Dickinson, Hippo, 1983.

Explores the perennial problem of keeping a bedroom tidy. A resourceful solo Mum, moody Alex and ethnically mixed neighbours are all well illustrated. Others in series.

NON-FICTION

HOUSES AND HOMES

Helen Barden, 'Starting Geography' Series, Wayland, 1992.

Good photographs, chosen from around the world, activities and a glossary that contains definitions in simple language.

HOMES IN HOT AND COLD PLACES

Simon Crisp, Wayland, 1994.

Good on heating and insulation.

AT HOME IN WORDS AND PICTURES

Ruth Thomson, Watts Books, undated.

No text, just clear photographs of objects in the home. Could be used for second language learners or for special needs children.

JOURNEYS

A Topic for Key Stage 2, Year 4

'Journeys' is one of the most common topics in junior schools. It can start from the familiar journeys from home to school, but can also offer the excitement of finding out about distant and unknown places. Most children now take holidays away from home, and many travel abroad and have experiences they can share of their own journeys. Travel is likely to become even more important in the course of their lifetimes. The topic can also provide a vehicle for encouraging international understanding and exploring ideas of stereotypes.

It offers opportunities for work in most curriculum areas and could cover work on transport, tourism, food, wildlife migration, refugees, explorers... In fact, it could be a problem keeping the project sufficiently focused.

CORE AND FOUNDATION SUBJECTS

In the example here, the school has decided that the topic should be used mainly as a vehicle for two National Curriculum subjects: Geography and History. As with most topics, language activities are built in throughout. It does not, of course, cover all the necessary elements of these two subjects for this year-group; other skills and areas of study would be included in other topics.

In Geography the topic centres around the theme of 'Environment' although other attainment targets are also planned for. In History the main focus is on changes in the local area since 1930 in relation to transport, linking with a later general topic on Britain since 1930. Other aspects of local history are studied in a later topic. Environmental issues are used as a link with the rest of the journeys topic.

As you will see from 'Planning considerations', it is expected that Maths and English will also play a part, although each will also be continuing with other aspects of their particular syllabus.

ENVIRONMENTAL EDUCATION

The planners have decided to use 'the environmental impact of travel' as a way of linking some of the activities and as a conscious plan to cover some of the knowledge, skills and attitudes in *Curriculum Guidance 7,* without sacrificing any of the knowledge content for the two key subjects. Because of this, a large number of the proposed activities could be considered 'environmental'; we have just picked out some of the key ones from our supposed student's six-week plan.

The environmental issues outlined below are confined to those related to transport and tourism, as this is what the topic plan focuses on. 'Transport' obviously includes energy use, but in this hypothetical school energy is dealt with in detail as a science-based topic in its own right, so here it is just touched on. Similarly, air pollution is dealt with in detail in a topic called 'Planet Earth'. As with 'My home, my street', not all the issues are suitable for Year 4 children, at least not in any detail. If you were to do a similar topic, you would choose what to include depending on the resources available, the age, sophistication and previous experience of the children, as well as on the specific requirements of your school's syllabus.

The issues

TRAVELLERS AND STAY-AT-HOMES

People nowadays travel much more than they ever have – for work, for leisure, for shopping – and in general, they travel longer distances. This isn't to say that long-distance travel is new. Around 1000 BCE the Polynesians made incredible voyages from New Guinea to Tonga and Samoa to find new homes; St Paul journeyed all round the eastern Mediterranean to spread the message of Christianity; and 16th century European explorers set off into the unknown and sailed around the world in search of excitement, knowledge, fame and wealth. Much of this travel is evidence of 'Europe's conquest of the world' which established the patterns of international trade and associated resource exploitation which exists today - between northern and southern hemispheres and between east and west Europe[1].

But in Europe, until Victorian times, most people stayed put. Many country dwellers rarely ventured beyond their own village and then only to the local market town. Their entertainment, clothes and food were all produced locally, and their relatives and friends were part of the same community. Any journey had to be undertaken on foot or, for the few who could afford it, on horseback on in a horsedrawn vehicle.

Such journeys had little impact on the environment. Roads were only a few metres wide and often unpaved. Horse manure – the waste from the fuel used – was quickly recycled. The impact of coaching inns hardly compares with that of motorway service stations.

WIDENING HORIZONS

It was the coming of the railways which made travel not just the preserve of the rich. Workers could live outside a town and travel in to their job; friends could visit friends in distant towns; outings and seaside holidays became commonplace. Unfortunately, alongside the social benefits came the environmental costs – the countryside was carved up, the trains were noisy and sooty. Communities in towns were split, houses were knocked down and others had trains thundering past their windows.

> " 'Well I won't meddle with 'em myself,' said Solomon, 'But some say this country's seen its best days, and the sign is, as it's being overrun with these fellows trampling right and left, and wanting to cut it up into railways; and all for the big traffic to swallow up the little, so as there shan't be a team left on the land, not a whip to crack.' "
>
> GEORGE ELIOT,
> MIDDLEMARCH

[1] For more on this see Year 501: The conquest continues, N Chomsky, Verso, 1993. By the term 'Europe' Chomsky includes the settled colonies most notably the USA.

Later, the invention of the bicycle further increased the mobility of the ordinary working people. In its early days it was used largely for recreation. Although heavy and clumsy, it helped foster the idea of travelling for fun and, in particular, got town dwellers out into the country (a trend which has continued with the car – on a peak summer Sunday, 18 million people visit the British countryside!).

> "He wheeled his machine up Putney Hill, and his heart sang within him... And at the top of the hill... Hoopdriver mounted... and began his Great Cycling Tour along the Southern Coast... A new delight was in his eyes, quite over and above the pleasure of rushing through the keen, sweet, morning air. He reached out his thumb and twanged his bell out of sheer happiness."
>
> H G WELLS,
> THE WHEELS OF CHANCE

Bicycles have always been the most fuel-efficient and environment-friendly means of transport and it wasn't long before commuters were using them to get to work. The exercise is good for the health, there are no pollutants, a bicycle does not take up much room, and is often quicker than a car. (A typical result for the annual 7 kilometre London rush hour transport race hour is 41 minutes for a car and 22 for a bike.) Cycling can, unfortunately, be dangerous, but when safe, pollution-free routes are provided, people do cycle. More than one million journeys are made each year along the $12^{1}/_{2}$ mile Bath to Bristol cycle route constructed by Sustrans.

MAN'S BEST FRIEND?

> "The meaning of the automobile is freedom, self-possession, self-discipline, and ease. In it the travelling coach is revived in all its poetic plenitude, but in a form endlessly enriched by the former's exquisite potential for intensified and simultaneously expanded gratification.... We will never run the risk of being locked in a (railway) compartment with insufferable people..."
>
> OTTO JULIUS BIERBAUM, 1903,
> QUOTED IN THE ECOLOGIST, VOL. 24, NO. 3.

The biggest transport revolution, of course, was brought about by the car. Invented in the 1880s, it was initially a great status symbol. Mass production, started in the 1930s by Henry Ford, gradually changed all that, although until recently, driving was still an occupation for men rather than women – another sign of status. There are now an estimated 550 million cars in the world. In the USA there are 550 cars for every thousand people; in China, at present, the figure is 0.7 per thousand, but the Government there plans to produce a million cars annually by the year 2000. The UK Government forecasts a doubling of car numbers here by 2025.

There is no doubt that the car has brought great benefits but costs have also been enormous. A few facts will sketch in the picture. The manufacture of cars uses 20% of the world's steel and 10% of its aluminium; a car produces three times its own weight in CO_2 each year; the incidence of asthma, closely linked by some with vehicle emissions, doubled between 1979 and '91; air pollution damages trees and buildings; only half of nine-year-olds are allowed to cross roads alone; every 50 minutes a car is produced that will kill someone; buildings near main roads have to be double-glazed against noise pollution; in Los Angeles, one-third of the land is taken up by roads and another third by parking spaces; Twyford Down in Hampshire, a site of historic, aesthetic and wildlife importance, is scarred by a new motorway...

> "I love cars. I loved my father's cars and my mother's cars... I adored and worshipped my MGB – I even polished the copper pipes on the engine. I love cars of all shapes and sizes. Cars are a good thing...The car is going to be with us for a very long time. We must start thinking in terms that will allow it to flourish."
>
> ROBERT KEY, TRANSPORT MINISTER, AUGUST 1993

Road transport uses three times the energy and eight times the amount of space compared with rail to move the same number of people or amount of freight, but still 80% of the staff at the Department of Transport are concerned with road building and vehicles. Experiments in places such as Zurich have shown that if public transport is cheap and reliable enough, people will use it in preference to their cars. After all, 61% of all car journeys are under 5 miles. Even in London, the GLC's aborted 'Fares Fair' policy decreased car use by 21%.

"So far I've spotted thirteen hedgehogs, four rabbits, a squirrel, three rooks, a chaffinch and a pied wagtail."

There are some encouraging signs. In 1994 the UK Government decided to cut back on its road-building programme; fewer out-of town shopping centres are being built; all European new cars must have catalytic converters; fuel-efficiency has become important in car design and new fuels are being investigated; but, car ownership is still encouraged as a matter of Government policy: *"The Government welcomes the continuing widening of car ownership as an important aspect of personal freedom and choice."*

> "I also love roads. I have always loved roads. Looking back on my childhood... I remember my father doing a diversion to Lincolnshire because he had heard there was some dual carriageway there..."
>
> ROBERT KEY, TRANSPORT MINISTER, AUGUST 1993

THIS COMMON INHERITANCE, BRITAIN'S ENVIRONMENT STRATEGY, 1990

THE SHRINKING WORLD

Rivalling the car in terms of its environmental impact is the wide-bodied jet aircraft. Its invention coincided with the advent of more money, more free time and a greater demand for 'recreation' by ordinary working people in the West. The aristocratic classes had always been able to travel; then in 1869 Thomas Cook arranged his first package tour for 'genteel adventurers' – a tour to Egypt. Now a holiday abroad is no longer a luxury; for many it is seen as an essential relief from the stresses of modern life. In 1960 worldwide there were 60 million international tourist arrivals. In 1990 it was over 400 million.

Aeroplanes themselves are very polluting and use huge quantities of fuel, but there are also severe environmental effects on the host country once the tourists arrive. Many countries, both 'first' and 'third' world, used to see tourism as a non-polluting industry which could bring quick wealth with little investment. It certainly is important economically: in 1989 it employed more people than any other industry in the world and foreign tourists spent over £100 billion, £8 million of it in Britain.

"If these Antarctic holiday tours catch on, this place is going to look like Blackpool beach in a few years time."

It is the very success of the industry which has brought the problems. Again, just a few facts can serve as an indication. In Nepal, widespread deforestation is the result of climbers needing fuelwood and in the Dominican Republic 1,000,000 trees were cut down to provide golf courses. The skiing industry has been responsible for severe erosion of The Alps and more frequent avalanches. Coral, which covers only 1% of the ocean floor, is home to 25% of marine species; coral reefs are protected in many areas, but still 2,000 tonnes are sold as souvenirs each year. In Greece and Turkey, the nesting sites of the endangered loggerhead turtle have been badly damaged by tourist development and in Hawaii the sacred sites of the indigenous people have been desecrated. And then there is water pollution, damage to ecosystems, air pollution, resource depletion, beach erosion...

TRAVEL BROADENS THE MIND?

The social effects are no less profound. People are disrupted from their traditional ways of life and their festivals and celebrations become shows for the visitors; farmers grow food and fishermen catch fish for the tourists instead of home consumption; rural dwellers leave the farms for the seaside resorts; peaceful villages become urbanised; and Western culture spreads inexorably – the 'coca-colarisation' of the world. Some travellers genuinely wish to learn about and from the cultures of other countries. There is an expansion of 'ecotourism', which places emphasis on the non-disruption of local life; but still for many tourists a trip abroad stresses the inequality of host and guest and reinforces cultural stereotypes.

Outline Topic Plan

Duration   6 Weeks

Years   4

Topic   Journeys

National Curriculum Subjects: Geography, History

Cross Curricular Themes: Environmental Education, Economic and industrial Understanding

School Resources Available: Large-scale local map, UK maps large world map, small world map stencil, globe, some photos of other countries, old and new photos of local area, *Learn to Travel* (WWF), books

Details of Subject Areas:

Geography
Skills: asking geographical questions about a place; geographical vocabulary; map skills with large- and small-scale maps and atlases; following routes, compass points, simple symbols and key; relationship between map and globe; use a variety of source material, including books and photos.

Places: General work on places, developing a locational framework in a world context: locating some of the places on the National Curriculum maps A, B and C; physical and human features and environmental issues; how places differ; relationship of features of locality and human activity; the geographical context.

Themes:
- communications: why, when and how people make journeys; different modes of transport and transport networks

- economic activities: land used in different ways and conflict over use (tourism v local activities)

- environment: human activities affect the environment; how and why people seek to manage and sustain the environment

History
Britain since 1930: changes in transport and its effects on people's lives

Local study: an aspect of the local community related to main study unit

Developing a sense of chronology; using historical dates and terms; examining reasons for and results of changes; using first hand evidence in the street and photographs as a historical source (local High Street).

Cross-Curricular Themes:
Environmental education – As well as the environmental geography, emphasise the skills and attitudes outlined in *Curriculum Guidance 7*. Use the environmental effect of travel as a link between the History and Geography parts of the topic.

Industrial and Economic Understanding – tourism as an industry – not a detailed study, but showing tourism from the point of view of the hosts as well as the guests.

Planning Considerations:

Three afternoons per week, plus relevant work in English and Maths sessions.

English – Opportunities for organised discussion, independent use of reference books, factual writing, story writing and producing some writing for display.

Maths – Opportunities for group and class graph-making.

History – In addition to main work, books on famous explorers should be available and one or two read at story time. Discuss racism, colonialism, Eurocentrism as appropriate.

Expected Outcomes:

Individual folders: including stories, map work and some evidence of research.

Display: local large-scale map with children's routes to school marked, colour-coded according to means of transport

Individual folders:

- memory map of journey to school - story about journey using lots of different transport - writing from 'Holiday brochure images' activity -
- maps of world with locations, routes and distances of the five holiday locations, Costa del Sol, Himalayas, Caribbean Islands, Rome, Scotland (ski resort);
  - newspaper report of meeting in 'Tropical beach hotel' - 'getting around' quiz sheet - 'timeline' worksheets - design for vehicle using renewable power
  - adventure story about journey

Display:

- class graphs 'How we come to school' and 'every type of transport we have used' - group wallcharts of 'methods of travel' and 'why people travel' - leaflets on study of transport (afterwards in folders) - group suggestions for improving congestion in High Street - class picture of 'Henry's Quest' - large world map, with the five holiday locations marked, and photos linked to location with coloured thread.

Five radio scripts and recordings:

- about five minutes, in the style of a radio or TV travel programme containing: general information about five holiday locations: information useful to tourists: information about the effects of tourism: pointers to being a good tourist.

Six week Topic Plan

SIX WEEKS TOPIC PLAN

Journeys

Week 1

Activity	Purpose	Notes	Advance Planning
Introduction	Introducing ideas about different reasons for travel, different methods, different destinations, different lengths. Introducing books for topic corner.	Whole class; teacher-led discussion based on children's experiences but bringing in wider examples.	Selection of books.
Pictorial memory maps of journey to school	Validating children's personal perceptions of local area. Beginning to consider differences in car and foot travel. Introduction to map-making.	Each child makes own map, then group and class discussion. Emphasise personal impressions, significant features, accuracy not important. In pairs or small groups of children who live near each other discuss reasons for differences, car/pedestrian etc. Finish with class discussion.	None.
Making wall charts – different methods of transport or why people travel	Organising information, writing and drawing for presentation. Collaboration. Consolidating learning about travel and transport and people's choices.	Small friendship groups, choose which of the two charts they want to do and decide what information to convey and how. Emphasise cooperation, splitting up tasks. Importance of presentation and layout.	None.

OTHER ACTIVITIES:

Route-finding game on large-scale local map – children give each other directions. Marking individual journey to school routes on map – colour-coded for means of transport. Picture graph of how we come to school. Graph of all methods of transport ever used by children and how many have used it. Children's and families' longer journeys, past and present – discussion with different scale maps. Individual story writing about an imaginary journey using lots of different types of transport.

SIX WEEKS TOPIC PLAN

Journeys

Week 2

Activity	Purpose	Notes	Advance Planning
Simplification of "Holiday brochure images" from "Learn to Travel".	Introduction to the five holiday locations and how they differ. Tourism as an industry; understanding what it is about an environment which attracts tourists. Appreciating the power of advertising; analysing and interpreting information.	Class, groups and individual work. Discussion, analysing text, individual writing, using brochures from the five holiday destinations.	Get holiday brochures. Select texts. Grade for difficulty.

OTHER ACTIVITIES:

Introducing tourism, discussion, teacher giving information and reading from reference book. Coloured pins on UK map of all places visited by children. Ditto on world map plus the five holiday destinations clearly marked. Starting group radio scripts for the five holiday destinations – use of brochures, discussion, notes, typing on computer.

PART 8

SIX WEEKS TOPIC PLAN

Journeys

Week 3

Activity	Purpose	Notes	Advance Planning
'Tropical beach hotel' from "Learn to Travel"	Awareness of place and how a location differs from home. Studying land use and conflicts arising; and provision of goods and services. Understanding that tourism is an industry and how it can affect an environment and local community. Fostering empathy with other people.	Role play in which children take the parts of members of a tropical community and of various vested interests who want to build a hotel.	Obtain beach scenes and hotel photos from brochures.
'Turkey's turtles' from "Learn to Travel"	Understanding the effects of tourism on environment and wildlife and how conflict arises over land use; how and why people seek to manage and sustain the environment. Reading with understanding.	Pairs do worksheet-guided research, class discussion.	Rewrite excerpts for easier reading level. Find pictures and other information. Prepare worksheets.
Environmental and social impacts of tourism	Collaborative, factual writing. Understanding the effects of tourism on environment and wildlife and how conflict arises over land use; suggesting solutions.	Class discussion, teacher information, group and individual research based on questions on worksheets. Different impacts of tourists, especially the five holiday locations. Share information from other sources. Groups write joint notes for radio script and two children type during week.	Find suitable pictures and information. Add to resource boxes where appropriate.

None.

SIX WEEKS TOPIC PLAN

Journeys

Week 4

Activity	Purpose	Notes	Advance Planning
Investigating ways of getting around	Understanding that different forms of travel have different impacts on the environment; why people choose different forms of travel; why different forms of travel are suitable for different places.	Class discussion and pairs quiz on worksheet. Quiz should require discussion and a little research.	Prepare quiz sheets and reference material.
Travel in our area, then and now	Investigating how and why transport has affected local area past and present.	Use photos of local area. Class discussion, then visit High Street. Groups compare old photos and present scene. How has local area changed? How has transport changed? What are the links? Different experiences offered by different transport; traffic problems in High St.	Get old photos of local area from resource store.

OTHER ACTIVITIES:

Marking routes to holiday destinations on large world map; environmental effects of plane travel. Other ways of crossing water. Travel section of radio scripts. Looking at railmaps of Britain, pre-war and present.

SIX WEEKS TOPIC PLAN

Journeys

Week 5

Activity	Purpose	Notes	Advance Planning
Improving traffic problem in High Street	Suggesting improvements to a local environmental problem. Use of large-scale map.	Class brainstorm, group collaborative writing and drawing. What causes the problem? Long-term/short-term solutions – traffic controls/better public transport etc. Use map. Children choose interest groups and work up solution. Continue next week if necessary.	None.

OTHER ACTIVITIES:

Adding any new information to and polishing radio scripts. General group investigation of history of transport in UK since 1930, using timeline worksheets and reference books.

Individual choice of mini-topic – use research skills as practised to produce information leaflet.

Read 'Henry's Quest', discuss life without petrol; why petrol makes emperor powerful.

SIX WEEKS TOPIC PLAN

Journeys

Week 6

Activity	Purpose	Notes	Advance Planning
Presenting local improvement suggestions	Suggesting improvements to local area. Following an argument, asking relevant questions and making constructive criticism.	After each group presentation, class comments and constructive criticism - of plans, not presentation.	None.
Designing a vehicle which doesn't use petrol	Designing to fulfil a need; drawing on information from other times; annotated drawings. Understanding difference between renewable and non-renewable resources; thinking about the future.	Refer to "Henry's Quest". Discussion and drawing. Petrol a finite source and polluting; renewable energy sources. Keep tone light. Drawings for fun, but should be thought out.	None.
Transport in the future	Understanding how and why people seek to manage and sustain the environment and considering the needs of future generations. Writing for presentation, reasoned arguments.	Discussion, writing, drawing. Environment-friendly transport; how to cut down travel; possible future of the types of transport researched – add to leaflets.	None.

Finish individual leaflets on transport since 1930. Recording and playing radio programmes.

Class mural of "Henry's Quest" – his journey. Children's own journey stories and pictures, possibly based on "Henry's Quest".

Session Plan 1

Week *One*

Activity Title: *Environmental and social aspects of tourism*

Date: *23rd September*   Time: *11.00 am*   Duration: *1 hour (continued in English session*

Group: *Class, then 5 groups*   Age: *Year 4*   Place: *Classroom*

Curriculum Focus:
Geography – how people affect the environment; how and why people seek to manage and sustain an environment; conflict over land use

English – group discussion; collaborative, factual writing; drafting and revising.

Preparation and Resources:
Contact Tourism Concern for possible case studies.
Find suitable pictures and information, e.g. from New Internationalist, National Geographic. Add to resource boxes where appropriate.
Make and photocopy five information/question sheets. Remember to grade for difficulty.
✱ Keep 'Spain' one very simple for special needs group.

Learning Objectives: (skills, knowledge, attitudes):
1 To raise awareness that tourism can have a marked impact on the people, environment and wildlife of the host country.
2 To gain information about the five holiday locations.
3 To empathise with people from other cultures, in other situations.
4 To share the information learned with others in the form of a 'radio' script.
5 To work collaboratively, sharing tasks and making joint decisions.

Activity Outline:
1 General discussion about the impact of tourism, focusing on five holiday locations.
2 Make joint list of the various kinds of impacts. See how they relate to five holiday locations.
3 Start groups off with their information and guidance sheets for writing their radio scripts.

Organisation of Children and Resources:
Start with children on mat. Use chalkboard for writing list.
Have resources to hand with markers in appropriate pages.
Children then divide into groups at tables, with worksheet.

Session Structure

1 Introduction

Find out what children already know about tourist impact from their own experience/reading/TV and from two previous sessions.

2 Development
General discussion, providing information where necessary, e.g. Hawaii facts and pictures from New Internationalist and some of the statistics on fact page. Remember age of children – keep simple.

What resources do tourists use? Where does the food come from? What other problems are caused? e.g. sewage disposal, wear and tear on natural environment, litter, what happens to local culture? What kind of souvenirs are good/bad to buy? How is wildlife harmed? What makes a good tourist?

Focus on five holiday locations so each group has one or two specific things to write about: litter on Mt Everest; overuse of fuelwood and trekkers' lodges built on grazing lands; sewage in the Mediterranean, threats to seals, forest fires; damage to Rome's ruins by people's feet and traffic congestion made worse by coaches; golf courses from farm and forest land in Caribbean and local life disrupted; ski resorts in Scotland in prime wildlife habitats, soil erosion and increased risk of avalanches?

Make 'webs' with children of the main dangers. Amend list as they make suggestions, so that it is not lots of specific examples but more general categories. (NB Rewrite on poster later and put on wall.) e.g.

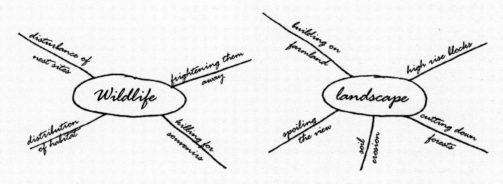

Hand out photocopied sheets. General questions which relate to the discussion and others about specific location, with pointers of where to look for further information in resource box, e.g. 'Some of the answers to these questions are on page 29 of The New Internationalist', starting and finishing where you see '. Look at the photographs on page 28 as well.

→ Lots of trees have been cut down in the Himalayas for tourists. Why do tourist need wood?

→ What harm does it do to the environment?

→ What other damage do tourists cause here?

→ How many tourists visit Northern Annapurna each year?"

3. Conclusion

No conclusion in this session. To be completed in English sessions, when children draft a script from their notes. Two children from each group (not the same two as last week) do final version on word processor as can be fitted in throughout week.

Evaluation:

Session Plan 2

Week Two

Activity Title: Travel in our area, then and now

Date: 30th September   **Time:** 1.20 pm   **Duration:** 2 hrs (extend over playtime)

Group: Class, 5 groups, class   **Age:** Year 4   **Place:** Classroom and outside – corner of High Street and Long Lane

Curriculum Focus:

History – an aspect of local history related to the study unit, 'Britain since 1930'
English – discussion skills

Preparation and Resources:

Two parents, auxiliary and class teacher needed
Brief helpers
Get photographs from resource store
Photocopy main photo
Polaroid camera
Clipboards
Large sheet of paper

Learning Objectives (skills, knowledge, attitudes):

1 To gain experience in interpreting pictures.
2 To appreciate that the local environment can be a learning resource.
3 To encourage children to feel part of a local and ongoing community.
4 To learn about the local area and transport since 1930.
5 To describe changes over a period of time and offer some reasons for such changes.
6 To recognise that over time some things change and some stay the same.
7 To identify different kinds of cause and effect, especially in relation to environment and how humans have had an impact on the environment, past and present.
8. To recognise the importance of planning, design and aesthetic considerations in the built environment.
9. To gain experience in expressing personal views.
10. To listen to and appreciate others' views.

Activity Outline:

1. Look at old photos of local area, focus on High Street photo.
2. Go out to same spot. Groups discuss changes in detail.
3. Return to classroom and compare notes. Discuss current difficulties caused by traffic at this spot.

Organisation of Children and Resources:

Start all together on mat. Groups for going out. Me to take blue group (most able), teacher greens (special needs). Other three to parents and auxiliary.
Clipboard and photocopy of photo for each group.

<u>Session Structure:</u>

<u>1. Introduction</u>

Children on mat. Show old photos of area. Ask if children can recognise where they are. See if they can recognise that they are from different periods. How do they know – what has stayed the same? What are the main differences? Which buildings have gone? How is the traffic different? Ask children to think about why changes have happened. Where might the people have been going? Long journeys or short journeys? Talk about what travel would have been like for people in the past. Point out horse-drawn bus. What would such a bus journey have been like? Read excerpt from book.

<u>2. Development</u>

Show 1920 photo of High Street and Long Lane. Ask if they can tell where it was taken from. Explain about trams. Explain that when we go out, children are to focus on changes due to changes in transport.

Get coats and divide into groups. Hand out clipboards and photocopies of photo. Remind children of rules for visits out.

With children, try to find exact spot photo was taken from. Divide into groups each with adult. Children to look for changes. Should notice types of vehicle, amount of traffic, relative proportions of buses/trams, commercial vehicles, bikes and private vehicles. Also ways of controlling traffic – road markings, bollards, parking signs, traffic lights, direction signs, zebra crossing. Make sure children talk about why the changes have occurred and not just what has changed.

My group take turns to note changes and comments on clipboard. Other groups dictate to adult. Take Polaroid photo.

Return to classroom. Locate photo spot and where we were standing on local map. Compare notes. On large sheet of paper make one column of mutually agreed list of changes and one of reasons.

Discussion: Do children think things were better then or now? In what ways? What were the good things and bad things about horsedrawn traffic? – For the travellers? For the environment? For the horses? Why were there more bicycles? What are the advantages and disadvantages of trams? Tell children about trams in European countries and new ones here. What could people do in the streets they can't do now? Give figures about children's independence. In what ways is it easier or better for people now? In what ways is it worse? What changes do they think there are which the photos don't show? (Air and noise pollution)

<u>3. Conclusion:</u>

What might the same spot look like in 50 years time? What would the children like it to look like? List suggestions.

<u>Evaluation:</u>

1. Suppose the school had wanted to use the topic to focus on Geography and Technology. Refer to the current Technology document, and write some notes on how aspects of the Technology curriculum could be covered in a topic on `Journeys', still keeping in mind the environment theme.

2. And now do the same for Science. If you can get a copy of the book used in this topic, "Henry's Quest" (see Resources, page 99) see if you can find ways of using it in connection with the Science curriculum.

3. Choose one of the activities in the six week topic plan which you think is relevant for environmental education and write up a session plan following the models here.

4. Many other activities are possible which relate journeys to environmental issues. Jot down any ideas which come to mind. What about for an older or younger age-group? It would be useful to keep – and add to – such jottings in a notebook, along with other topics, for future reference.

RESOURCES

Curriculum Materials

GREEN TRANSPORT PACK

WWF-UK/Transport 2000/Environmental Transport Association/Hovis National Bike Week, 1993. Available from WWF.

A slim book packed with information and ideas for activities with primary school children. Highly recommended.

LEARN TO TRAVEL

Peter Mason, WWF-UK, 1992.

This is the book from which three of the activities are taken. 'Turkey's Turtles' involves research about the endangered loggerhead turtles under threat from tourism on Turkey's beaches. 'Tropical beach hotel' is a role play in which the situation is that a large hotel is to be built on a fishing beach in a developing country. The characters are from the local community, local government, tourist company and tourists themselves. "Holiday brochure images" encourages critical reading and writing.

NEW INTERNATIONALIST

No. 245, July 1993. Available from NI, (Back Copies) 55 Rectory Road, Oxford OX4 1BW, price £1.50.

The whole issue is devoted to tourism, particularly its impact on the 'third world'. For adults, but you could make use of some of the information and selected extracts with children.

NEW JOURNEYS

Birmingham Development Education Centre, 1992. Available from Birmingham DEC, Gillett Centre, 998 Bristol Road, Selly Oak, Birmingham B29 6LE. Also available from Oxfam. £15.50.

This pack, compiled by a group of primary school teachers after a study visit to Kenya and Tanzania, includes photographs, a map and suggestions for activities. A large section is devoted to the issue of tourism.

QUESTIONING TOURISM

Commonwealth Institute/Focus for Change, 1990. Available from The Commonwealth Institute, 230 Kensington High Street, London W8 6NQ. Also available from Oxfam. £4.00.

A pack containing photocopyable sheets exploring the costs and benefits of tourism, particularly in developing countries. Where possible, the materials relate to the children's own experiences as both tourists and hosts.

Fiction and Non-fiction Books

FICTION

HENRY'S QUEST

Graham Oakley, Macmillan Children's Books 1986.
This is the book used in the topic plan. Set in the future, it tells the story of a peaceful country in the depths of the forest. There are clues to life in times past – a cooker abandoned in the undergrowth, cars used as chicken coops... The king sends knights off on a quest for an unknown thing called 'petrol'. Henry, a shepherd, joins the quest. His journey takes him through the forest where there are more signs of a past civilisation – broken motorways, people living in jumbo jets, petrol stations used as cow sheds. Transport now is by bike and horsedrawn wagons (old trucks). After an eventful journey, Henry overthrows a tyrant ruler in a decadent city, finds some petrol and returns in triumph, with two cans, to claim his reward.

LEGENDS OF JOURNEYS

Olga Norris, Cambridge University Press, 1988.
An excellent collection with a variety of stories from around the world, well suited for primary children.

MRS ARMITAGE ON WHEELS

Quentin Blake, Puffin 19??.
Mrs Armitage keeps adding things to her bike until she crashes. She then starts again with roller skates. Easy to read and good fun.

OVER THE GREEN HILLS

Rachel Isadora, Julia Macrae, 1992.
Zolani and his mother set off one morning to walk many miles to visit grandma with gifts of food. The beautiful paintings of Transkei life and landscape are accompanied by simple text full of love and friendship.

ON YOUR CYCLE

Michael, Vernon Scannell, Red Fox, 1992.
(First published 1991 by Bodley Head under the title Travelling Light.)
A collection of comic poems about every kind of travel from prams to rockets. Children will have great fun listening to them, and some might even be encouraged to learn one – perhaps for an assembly or other presentation of the work on journeys?

NON-FICTION

CARS

Ruth Thomson, 'Changing Times' series, Franklin Watts, 1992.
Looks at the recent past through the eyes of four generations of a real family. Simple text, excellent photographs and contemporary illustrations.

EXPLORING TRANSPORT

Cliff Lines, 'Exploring the Past' series, Wayland 1988.
Photographs and contemporary illustrations accompany a text which some Year 4 children should be able to tackle. It concentrates on transport in Britain, encouraging children to look for clues to times past, and also offers other suggestions for activities.

JOURNEYS

Julia Waterlow, 'Young geographer' series, Wayland, 1993.

JOURNEYS

Helen Barden, 'Starting Geography' series, Wayland, 1992.
Two very similar books, both with a simple text and plentiful photographs and both covering ideas about why and how people round the world make journeys. Useful as an introduction.

MAPS AND JOURNEYS

Kate Petty, A & C Black, 1993.
Simple text linked to illustrations clearly explains difficult ideas. Activities help young children to follow a route, identify landmarks and learn important geographical vocabulary.

ON THE ROAD

John Baines, 'The Green Detective' series, Wayland, 1992.
Plenty of ideas here for children – and you – about the issues of road transport and the environment. Accessible information, activities, fact boxes, and things to think about make it a mini-project in itself.

RAILWAYS

Althea and Edward Parker, 'Built with a purpose' series, A & C Black.
Traces the development of railways from earliest times till now. The style is friendly and accessible, and the illustrations and photographs helpful.

Addresses

ADDRESSES

BICYCLE ASSOCIATION

Stanley House, Eaton Road, Coventry CV1 2FH.
This is the trade association for the bicycle industry but they do have useful information leaflets and a teaching pack. This is aimed at upper juniors and lower secondary, but many of the activities could be adapted for younger children and there are four very appropriate posters.

GREEN FLAG INTERNATIONAL

PO Box 396, Linton, Cambridgeshire, CB1 6UL.
Primarily an organisation which helps the travel and tourism industry to 'go green', it also has a few publications useful for the general public. These include a leaflet, *A Travellers Guide to Tourism* and a paper, *What is a Green Holiday?*. Available free but a stamped, addressed A4 envelope would be appreciated.

SUSTRANS

35 King Street, Bristol BS1 4DZ. Tel: 01179 268893.
Builds traffic-free routes – Greenways – for pedestrians and cyclists using disused railway lines, towpaths, forest tracks etc.

TRANSPORT 2000

Walkden House, 10 Melton Street, London NW1 2EJ.
A federation of various groups which campaigns for a coherent and sustainable national transport policy which meets transport needs with the least damage to the environment. Contact them for current publications or information. For example, in 1993 they produced an action pack to support Green Transport Week.

TOURISM CONCERN

Southlands College, Roehampton Institute, Wimbledon Parkside, London SW19 5NN
As well as its campaigning work, through its membership network, global contacts and resource collection, Tourism Concern is a centre of advice and imformation on tourism's impact.

FOOD

A Topic for Key Stage 2, Year 6

Very often a school will have a topic which the whole age-range studies at the same time, with each year or class focusing on a different aspect or curriculum area. 'Food' is one such topic, because it offers such a wide range of activities and levels of interest, and can always be rooted in the children's own experience. In our example, the topic lasts just four weeks, but takes up more of the timetable than is usual for a single subject. Geography and History would not be studied at all during this time – they might have their own period of intense work at some other time. This is another common pattern of topic work in junior schools.

Other year-groups would be covering cooking and the social aspects of food, packaging and advertising, cooking and physical processes, world food distribution and famine, and diet and health. On the last day, each class holds open house, where they display, explain and demonstrate what they have been doing to parents, other guests and the rest of the school.

CORE AND FOUNDATION SUBJECTS

For Year 6 this is a single subject topic – Science – although Maths, English and IT will be involved in the measuring and recording of experiment results. There is also a small overlap with Geography in the farm visit which 'our' student develops to include some investigation of human impact on the environment.

The Science focuses on plants as organisms and conditions necessary for growth, with emphasis on the procedures of scientific investigation, and on food chains. A lot of the work would be spread out over the weeks; measuring or drawing plant growth, for example, may only take a few minutes, but needs to be done at regular intervals. (In four weeks, growth can be studied only in plants which germinate and grow quickly, but when you have your own class, there may be more opportunity for examining plant growth over a longer period.)

ENVIRONMENTAL EDUCATION

Unlike the previous two topics, the outline plan prepared by the school does not include any specific reference to environmental issues. However you will see from the detailed plan excerpts that our hypothetical student has seen ways of including issues of sustainability without neglecting the curriculum targets. The emphasis is on the harm modern farming methods, particularly the use of agrichemicals, can do to the natural environment. (This is, in fact, a requirement at Key Stage 3, when it will be studied in more depth.) But notice that there is no intention here to 'hi-jack' the topic for Environmental Education; it is just one small component in a Science topic.

PART 9

FEEDING THE HUNGRY?

After the Second World War there was a great drive in Europe and other countries to increase food production. In some developing countries it became an urgent necessity because of rapidly rising populations. India doubled its wheat crop in 15 years and many Western farmers produce twice as much food on the same amount of land as they did 30 years ago. In fact, in Europe this led to the much-publicised lakes and mountains of surplus food and drink.

These huge increases have been achieved in a number of ways: larger fields and machines, improved irrigation, temperature control (in greenhouses and so on), selecting breeds, gene engineering, feed supplements, intensive animal husbandry and, above all, through the use of agrichemicals – fertilisers and pesticides.

It may seem like a triumph that so much extra food has been produced and we must not knock the achievement of dedicated farmers and scientists. But there have been costs. In the South it has been largely the richer land-owners who have benefitted because peasant farmers could not afford the machinery, chemicals and special high-yielding varieties of seeds. Modern farming methods not only need more capital – which is in short supply in developing countries – but need less labour – which is plentiful. The poor thus lose out both ways. There has been a marked trend towards growing cash crops, especially for the export market, and away from food the local people can actually eat. So many may be hungrier than before. The impact on animal welfare is now well known: veal crates, battery hens and BSE. However, this school topic is about crops rather than animals.

> "...a fundamental relationship between human beings and their environment is that of their dependence on soil. We are reminded of this with every meal we eat every day of our lives. But as our way of life becomes more technologically determined, more urban, more 'advanced', so our distance from the soil grows."
>
> ROY WILLIAMS,
> ONE EARTH, MANY WORLDS

THE (LITERAL) LOSS OF THE COUNTRYSIDE

All over the world, intensive farming has led to soil erosion on a vast scale. Large fields, lack of hedges and trees, no renewal of the humus in the soil and constant ploughing all allow the wind to whisk up the top layers and deposit them in the sea. On the Sussex Downs the annual loss has been recorded as 200 tonnes per hectare!

Irrigation can also lead to loss of fertile soil, but in a different way. Where the land does not drain properly, the water evaporates and salts build up in the topsoil, making it impossible for plants to grow. This is already happening in some of the seemingly lush valleys of California.

MAGIC DUST?

Not so long ago, the only nutrients put into the soil came from plants and animals. Nowadays nitrogen, phosphorous and potassium are mined or manufactured and used as fertiliser, greatly boosting crop yields – and weeds. So herbicides must be used. The lush growth is not only attractive to humans; aphids also love it. So – pesticides.

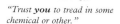

The nitrates in the fertiliser don't all get used by the plants, so a lot leaches out and gets into the rivers, where it encourages very fast algae bloom. As the algae decomposes, it uses up oxygen (eutrophication) which means that fish and other aquatic life are deprived of it and die.

*"Trust **you** to tread in some chemical or other."*

The nitrates also get into our drinking water supplies and they are known to cause cancer. In the last 20 years nitrate levels in many ground and surface waters have risen between 50 and 400%. In 1992 Britain was convicted by the European Court of Justice for failing to meet health standards for nitrates in drinking water in 28 areas. Water companies do spend huge amounts trying to remove the nitrates, but not much on tackling the problem at source. In 1990-91 the Government gave farmers in 'Nitrate Sensitive Areas' £600,000 to clean up their act. However, it also gave £1,663,000,000 on price support to conventional farming (rather than organic), thereby supporting the over-use of nitrates.

PESTICIDES - BOON OR BANE?

This depends on who you are. If you are a shareholder in a multinational chemical company you are probably laughing. If you are a farmer, a jogger, a new-born baby, or if you drink UK water you may not be so happy.

The issues (cont)

One billion gallons of pesticide are sprayed on Britain each year and 600 different types are permitted in the EC.

Alar, banned in the USA as a carcinogen and now withdrawn world-wide by the makers, passed British safety tests.

Farmers who use herbicides frequently are eight times more likely to get non-Hodgkins lymphoma (a cancer) than average.

In one survey 10% of UK lettuces contained residues indicating 'a misuse of pesticides', according to a leaked memo from MAFF.

The Environmental Working Group (USA) report that a child aged one could easily have received a maximum life-time's dose for eight pesticides from just 20 commonly eaten foods.

A report from HM Agricultural and Factory Inspectorate in 1989–90 confirms that forty-three people were poisoned by pesticides. A quarter were affected while walking or jogging by a sprayed field.

300 drinking water supplies in Britain have breached EC limits for pesticides residues.

In 1992, £450 million was spent on reducing pesticides residues in our water supplies.

The BMA says that even breast milk can exceed the maximum residue level permitted for pesticides, so persistent are they in the body.

A pesticide called methyl bromide is thirty times more destructive to the ozone layer than CFCs.

The government does, of course, control the testing, sale and use of pesticides, but many people feel that too many accidents happen and that current testing does not take enough account either of the long-term effects of low dosage or of the mixtures of chemicals which can inadvertently occur when many different ones are used in the same area. Also, new chemicals are constantly having to be produced as pests become resistant to them, so adding to the cocktail.

THE POISON SPREADS

"In 1988, 1,685 insects, 149 plant, 51 bird and 24 butterfly species were endangered, rare or vulnerable in the UK. 10 plant and 1 butterfly species have become extinct in the last 40–50 years."

SOIL ASSOCIATION, 1993

Pesticides obviously kill pests, but those pests are lunch for ladybirds, badgers, frogs... If the pest dies out, predators go hungry. In addition, if the pest gets eaten before it dies, the poison may not break down in the body and so it will spread up through the food chain. The American robin very nearly died out through eating worms poisoned with DDT before the chemical was banned. The further up the chain the animal is, the more poison it will have in its body, because it will have eaten many smaller creatures.

Herbicides kill not only the weeds amongst the crops, but they drift and destroy nearby wild flowers. These are in turn food for insects which are themselves food for other creatures. In one recorded instance the survival rate for partridge chicks went up by three times when the adjacent field margins were not sprayed.

The issues (cont)

THE ANSWER?

In this country we do have National Nature Reserves, Country Stewardship Schemes and an increasing number of Environmentally Sensitive Areas in which farmers can claim Government subsidies for managing their land in a way that protects habitats. More and more farmers, both here and in the majority world, are going further and showing an interest in organic methods, although in the UK the total acreage of organic cropping is still less than 1% of the whole.

Basically, organic farming avoids the problems of conventional farming outlined above. It reduces soil, water and atmospheric pollution; conserves habitats such as pastures, hedges, ditches and trees; increases insect levels and hence mammals and birds; maintains diversity of flora; and, it could be argued, improves the scenic value of the countryside through smaller fields, hedges and the diversity of crop rotation. Above all, organic farming looks after the soil, seeing it not just as a medium for crops to root in, but as the most vital part of a living system.

Organic farming does not mean letting nature have its way. It needs very careful management. Crop rotation breaks the cycle of weeds and pests, and allows recovery from demanding crops. In fact, some crops, such as green manures and legumes, are grown specifically to put nitrogen back. Crop residues, animal manure and composting are also used to enrich the soil. Using natural predators and companion planting help to keep pests at bay. If a crop is actually in danger, then some plant or mineral based pesticides may be used.

Nitrate pollution from organic farming "will be minimal compared to the pollution that will come from normal conventional farming."

DAVID TRIPPER,
MINISTER OF STATE FOR
THE ENVIRONMENT AND
COUNTRYSIDE, 1992

Sounds all too good to be true? Well, organic food is more expensive, although this is partly owing to heavy subsidies for conventional farming – a position which may be changing. Organic farming is also labour intensive and the work may be more arduous. Crop yields are generally not so high, although some organic farmers might dispute this – and anyway, in Europe we produce too much food. With so much farming land now being 'set aside' for non-agricultural purposes because of this over-production, many would argue that it would make sense to cultivate less intensively and instead farm in a more environment-friendly way.

Outline Topic Plan

Duration   4 Weeks

Topic Food   **Years** 6

National Curriculum Subjects: Science. Also some IT and Geography.

Cross Curricular Themes: Economic and Industrial Understanding.

School Resources Available: Trays for seed growing, plant propagators, measuring jugs, etc, in Science cupboard; software – Data Handling in Primary Science; food chain worksheets, farm visit maps. Money for seeds, etc, available.

Details of Subject Areas:

Details of Subject Areas:

Science
As this is part of school 'Food' topic, concentrate on food plants in experiments.
Skills: planning experimental procedures, carrying out fair tests, obtaining and recording evidence, analysing evidence, drawing conclusions and considering evidence.

Plants as organisms – plants make food using energy from sun; the importance of leaves in this process; plant growth is affected by availability of light and water and by temperature; the function of the roots; the life cycle of plants.

Living things in their environment: most food chains start with green plants and show feeding relationships in an ecosystem; that micro-organisms exist and can be beneficial in breaking down waste.

IT
Some results should be recorded and analysed on the computer. The children have used this programme before.

Geography
On the farm visit there will be an opportunity to discuss land use.

Cross-Curricular Themes:

Farming as an industry. Not a major part of the topic.

Planning Considerations:

Two to three afternoons per week, plus relevant work in English and Maths sessions.

A farm visit is arranged for Week 3.

English – There will be ample opportunities for clear recording and other factual writing. Presentation will be very important because of the final 'open house'.

The final day is 'Open House' when parents and the other children will visit. Work needs to be displayed and the children prepared to explain and demonstrate as necessary.

Set up room as a laboratory with white coats, gloves and folders for each child with dividers labelled Experiments, Farming, Looking at plants, Soil, Food chains. There will be a lot of independent group work, so make sure each group has its tasks clear and keeps records, not just of experiments, but also of which tasks it has carried out and which need to be done.

Collect beans, cress seeds, assorted seed packets, science equipment, plastic gloves, plant propagator, growing medium (non-peat), books; arrange for children to bring clear plastic bottles to be cut down for growing beans, old white shirts for lab coats.

Each week there will be one or two interactive displays for children to work at in spare time.

Expected Outcomes:

Individual folders with:
- experiment records: computer printouts, drawings, written records
- food chain worksheets
- farm visit worksheets and maps

Room set up as laboratory:
- murals
- experiments displayed, clearly labelled, with results

Displays:
- seeds and packets
- sorting plants – various
- which part of plants do we eat?
- soil sorting
- food webs

Four week Topic Plan

SIX WEEKS TOPIC PLAN

Food

Week 1

Activity	Purpose	Notes	Advance Planning
Setting the scene	Introduction to rigorous scientific method. Developing ability to take charge of their own learning and think for themselves. Co-operative decision-making.	Me in role as 'head of laboratory'. Children to be research groups; each group to choose name, make folders badges; lab. procedures – wearing white coats, plastic gloves. Emphasise experimental procedures and that children are in charge. Introduce experiment task cards and equipment storage.	See planning considerations, plus make experiment task cards. All equipment, seeds, apples etc stored or displayed properly.
Factors affecting growth and germination	Investigating first hand factors that affect plant growth, including pollution; begin investigation of decay. Planning and carrying out fair tests, choosing suitable equipment and recording methods.	Start two groups at a time. Each group makes joint decision on which experiments, one first day, one second day – water, light, heat, fertiliser, acid (vinegar), indoor and out, type of soil or other growing medium. Two groups can choose same test, but do on different days.	As before.
Decay experiment	To demonstrate how food decays under a variety of circumstances, helping understanding of food chains later in project.	Class discussion of setting up fair test. Pieces of apple buried, left on different surfaces, etc.	Apples and knives.

OTHER ACTIVITIES:

Making folders, painting murals to make room look like laboratory, group badges, labels.

Entering parameters on computer. Individual 'planting' beans in plastic bottles.

Display of food packages: 'Look at the ingredients. What plants have gone into these foods?'

SIX WEEKS TOPIC PLAN

Food

Week 2

Activity	Purpose	Notes	Advance Planning
Visit from health food shop owner	Learning about conditions for plant growth; human impact on the environment. Following an argument and asking relevant questions. Meeting someone from local community.	Speaker to explain why she stocks organic vegetables. Pros and cons of organic farming – pollution, wildlife, landscape, soil, future.	Arrange visit, brief speaker.
Organic farming display	Recap and build on visitor's talk.	Interactive display of books and list of questions. No writing, just discussion. Individuals, pairs or groups, throughout week.	Write questions, display books.

OTHER ACTIVITIES:

Continuing and monitoring experiments, bean growth and decay. Investigating and comparing seeds, using seeds and information on packets. Preparing for farm visit.

SIX WEEKS TOPIC PLAN

Food

Week 3

Activity	Purpose	Notes	Advance Planning
Farm visit	Practising field work skills including maps. Learning about factors affecting plant growth. Investigating land-use distribution – what and why; human impact on the environment. Introduction to farming as an industry.	Discuss worksheets in pairs, complete individually. Follow maps.	Prepare maps and worksheets from discussion last week, three ability levels.
Food web game	Understanding food chains and interdependence of life – ecosystems; pollution from chemicals spreads up or disturbs food chain. Co-operation between children.	Play game as whole class. Groups and individuals do follow-up work.	Make organism list – what eats what. Balls of wool. Make headbands.

OTHER ACTIVITIES:

Continuing and monitoring experiments and bean growth. Checking the extent of decay in apples experiment. The form and function of roots. Comparing soils (from 'Food, farms and futures'). Interactive display: 'Which part of the plant do we eat?'

SIX WEEKS TOPIC PLAN

Food

Week 4

Activity	Purpose	Notes	Advance Planning
Sustainable farming in developing countries	Reading with understanding. Appreciating other cultures and realising that problems and solutions of farming are world-wide. Learning more about what is meant by 'sustainability'.	Upper ability groups only. Each group has a case study from 'Living Earth' and devises a comprehension which other groups then complete.	Prepare case studies.
Organic versus conventional farming debate	Consolidation of learning for whole class. Preparing arguments, listening, public speaking, expressing opinions.	During 'Open House', with parents and other children present and taking part if they wish. Remember consumer point of view – price, appearance, availability; farming as an industry.	Help main speakers prepare speeches, divide up points between them.

OTHER ACTIVITIES:

Stems, leaves and flowers. All plant growth experiments finished, recorded, analysed, compared. Final report on decaying apples. Prepare presentations for 'Open House'. Interactive display of lots of food – raw/dried/packets/tins etc. 'Sort these foods in any way you like. Ask other children to work out your categories.' Open House.

Session Plan

Activity Title: Food web game, (adapted from 'Food, Farms and Futures')

Date: 23rd June   **Time:** 1.30pm   **Duration:** 1 1/2 hours

Group: Class, then group and   **Age:** Year 6   **Place:** Classroom, then hall
individual   or playground,
depending on weather

Curriculum Focus:

Science – food chains

Preparation and Resources:

Strips of sugar paper, one for each child, with names of organisms written in large letters:
human, badger, hedgehog, bluetit, fox, stoat, eagle, kestrel, owl, shrew, mole, mouse, rabbit,
sheep, pheasant, robin, thrush, frog, ladybird, spider, worm, aphid, grasshopper, grass,
vegetables, seeds, nuts, decomposers, messenger
List of these organisms in order
✳Torch ✳Balls of old wool ✳Several rolls sticky tape ✳PE hoop ✳Large stand-up label 'soil'

— Draw and cut out pictures of food pyramid copied from 'Food, Farms and Futures'
— Two kinds of worksheet
— Check wildlife encyclopaedia to remind myself what all the animals eat

Learning Objectives:

1. To understand how a food chain operates.
2. To understand that plants use the energy of the sun to make food.
3. To begin to appreciate that life is a continuous cycle.
4. To see, by making a physical model, how all life is interconnected and begin to understand what an ecosystem is.
5. To group animals into herbivores, omnivores and carnivores and to understand the meaning of 'predator'.
6. To understand how pollution can affect the survival of organisms, and how poisons can have widespread effects.
7. To play a game in a spirit of co-operation.

Activity Outline:

Discuss what each animal eats, and role of decomposers.
- Play game.
- Introduce idea of poisons at one part of food chain. Discuss how poisons can accumulate in the food chain.

Organisation of children and resources

Whole class. Start on mat. Have sticky tape ready to make headbands. Take hoop, soil label, wool and list to hall or playground. Chart in classroom for return. Finish with group and individual work.

Session Structure:

1. Introduction

Introduce idea of what animals as well as humans eat. Show animal strips one by one, discuss/tell briefly what each one eats. Show plant strips. Where do plants get their food? Explain what decomposers are (fungi, bacteria, other soil organisms) and what they do. Importance of soil. Make clear that the plants don't actually eat the decomposers. Introduce idea of plants using energy from the sun to make food.

2. Development

1. Choose a competent reader for the messenger and Karen (needs confidence boost) as the 'decomposers'. Turn rest of strips face down, each child takes one. Help each other make headband with sticky tape. Go to hall or playground. Children sit in circle in order on list – don't tell them why. Place hoop as part of circle, with soil label. 'Decomposers' sits in hoop to show importance. Give messenger torch.

2. Explain game: Messenger gives one end of wool to 'decomposers', who sends it via the messenger to any plant. Messenger shines torch on 'plant' to represent sun. That plant chooses who to be eaten by. Can be helped to choose by person on either side (if help too general, will probably end up with shouting). Messenger gives ball of wool to that person who chooses again. Plant holds loop of wool while messenger takes the ball to next person, and so on. Anyone can choose to die and return to soil/decompose instead of being eaten. Decomposers always send wool to a plant.

3. Play game. Messenger must tread very carefully over wool to avoid tripping. Discuss when appropriate where the carnivores send the wool (but don't use word yet).

4. When everyone has been 'eaten' at least once and preferably more, stop for discussion. Children lay down wool very carefully and stand up. Can they see any pattern? Did the wool ever go from the plants to the group fox/stoat/eagle/kestrel/owl? Can they see which group of animals only eat plants? Sit down and continue discussion, illustrating with messenger and groups standing up, where necessary. Introduce words 'omnivore' (human, badger, hedgehog, bluetit), 'carnivore' and 'herbivore' (insectivore?)

5. Pretend to be farmer with insecticide. Explain what it is for, and why farmers use it, then 'spray' all the invertebrates. (Explain that in real life, one insecticide would not actually kill all kinds of invertebrates.) These children lie down. Now try to play the game again. Discuss the significance. What will happen to those creatures that feed on the insects?

3 Conclusion

Gather up wool, collect headbands, return to classroom. Explain that pesticide doesn't kill immediately and insect may get eaten before it dies. Show the one cut-out caterpillar. So what happens to the poison? Explain, with pictures, that a bluetit might eat 20 caterpillars in a day and a sparrowhawk eat two bluetits. What happens to the poison?

Special needs group work with teacher making simple food webs with pictures and wool for wall display. Most children start worksheet recapping points from lesson; most able do worksheet which also introduces idea of herbicides and how they interrupt the food chain. Can be finished later.

Evaluation:

Planning a farm visit

A well planned school visit can do more than anything else to motivate children in their topic. Often, the visit is planned as an integral part of the topic, as experience has shown that the effort and expense is well worth while. If you, as a student working with the class, can take responsibility for organising the trip, this will be a great boost to your confidence and to your esteem in staff room and college alike! And remember that although you may have organised the whole day, you will not ultimately be responsible for the children; the staff who come with you are still 'in charge', which will relieve your anxieties.

For this topic on 'Food', a visit to an arable farm would be invaluable. As well as seeing food growing, children would be able to link their small classroom experiments with real crops in real fields. The steps outlined below will help you either think about a trip or plan one in reality.

PRE-PLANNING THE WORK

As the visit is such a central part of the topic, the learning objectives should be quite apparent, but you still need to make yourself a detailed list. Refer to your topic sessions as well as the National Curriculum. Your list might look like this:

Science: conditions for growth

a) what does farmer do about soil, water?

b) does he use fertiliser? What? How much? Cost?

c) herbicides? What for? Damage to plants if not used? How much?

d) ditto for pesticides

e) wildlife and food chains

Geography: looking at land use

a) size of farm, size of fields

b) what crops, how often? anything new?

c) use of buildings

d) human impact on the environment

Cross-curricular skills

a) study of environment at first hand

b) active participation in resolving environmental problems (to be done later in school debate).

Other pre-planning: find clipboards and pencils, get film for camera, first aid bag, bucket and towels, spare clothing for young children.

Worksheets: not too difficult; include drawing or labelling parts of a drawing for less able. Be prepared to abandon if wet.

Plan a session with the class in which you detail the purpose of trip, timetable, their responsibility to behave appropriately, what they need to bring. Compile a list of questions for the farmer, and note points to be incorporated in worksheets.

PRE-VISIT TO THE FARM

The school may well have regular contact with a particular farm, but if you have to find one, use information from an agricultural association (see resources list) or see if the local education authority keeps a list of willing farmers. Write to the farmer and arrange a preliminary visit. You will probably go with a member of staff, but there is no reason why you shouldn't take the lead in talking to the farmer. Discuss your objectives and draw up a timetable for the day. Think about the following:

a) crops, machinery, size of fields, uses of buildings, use of chemicals, number of workers, pattern of year, where produce goes

b) what concepts and knowledge are fundamental for the children to learn?

c) how will the children move around the farm: groups?

d) potential dangers

e) somewhere for eating lunch, contingency arrangements for wet day, toilets.

It is easy to get sidetracked during an exciting visit. Remember, in this case, the topic is about plants as food, so you would have to politely decline the farmer's offers to show cows being milked or pigs fed. Similarly you would need to keep your own questioning focused on arable farming. You might have to explain the sort of information you were hoping to find: for example, you could show a food chain diagram to explain what the children need to think about. Be definite about your plans and try to make a good impression. If your class is also studying organic farming, be careful not to imply any criticism of a conventional farmer.

LEGAL REQUIREMENTS

It is essential that you get to know the education authority policy for school visits. This will include rules for the ratio of children to adults, the number of children on a coach and the manner in which parents give permission for their children to go on the trip. In most authorities the permission has to be in writing, and schools have a recommended form that they use. If the child loses a form you must be firm and insist on written permission; a phone call will not do. Schools are not allowed to charge for outings now, so the money has to be asked for in terms of 'a donation towards the costs'. Most schools will have a fund to help families on restricted budgets and you can ask the class teacher how to arrange this. If you expect to return to school after the normal going home time, the form should include a space for parents to say that they agree to collect their children at the stated time. No child should be left to go home on his/her own.

The letter to parents

Include:

Destination; time of departure and return; what the purpose is; what the children will need (clothing, footwear, lunch, drink in spill-proof container, camera), donation, slip to be filled in by parent giving permission for child to leave the school premises and agreeing to collect child at end of trip.

NB Present safety belt law is being changed, and some parents are worried that coaches and mini-buses still do not have belts for each child. They may suggest that they take children in their own cars. This looks like a good alternative, but warn them that they must have insurance to cover such use. Unless the whole class goes in cars you may be left in the position of having to hire a bus just to take a few children which will be impossibly uneconomic. This is a problem area at the moment, and we can only hope that belts will soon be compulsory in all public hire vehicles.

Parent helpers

One of the writers of this book on a school visit, after noticing that a group of children were wandering about without an adult, found the parent helper asleep on the back seat of the coach. She explained that she had been on night duty at the hospital and had had no sleep, but hadn't wanted to let the school down! It makes a good story, but how can you avoid this kind of fiasco?

Here are several useful tips.

a) Choose parents with a good track record of reliable help. If a parent is a first-time volunteer, pair them with someone else. This can be difficult because there is often a shortage of parents who are available during the day.

b) Hold a meeting before the trip in which you explain the nature and purpose of the visit, show the worksheets, go through the timetable. Make sure that they all recognise that the day is part of the school's work and that school discipline is expected.

c) Explain briefly the kinds of questions the adults could ask the children. Parents are diffident about mentioning their skills, so you might find that there are people who have a farming background, but only if you ask.

d) Give the helpers lists of the names of the children in their group. You may feel happier if you keep any 'problem' children in your group or the class teacher's.

e) Don't forget grandparents.

ON THE DAY

1. Take the register.

2. Put the children in groups with their helpers who have all arrived at the stated time (you hope!). Helpers check lunch bags.

3. Take first aid, bucket, paper towels, school camera, your own food (and a bit extra), spare pants and shorts for young children.

4. Leave register, list of helpers, address and phone number of farm, address and phone number of coach company with headteacher.

5. Before leaving coach, give out worksheets, clipboards and pencils, and go through final instructions.

6. During the day keep your eyes open for any possible problems, but try to remain relaxed.

7. Get back, see children off the premises, thank helpers, go to staff room and sink into chair!

FOLLOW-UP

Write, and encourage children to write, thank you letters to farmer and to parent helpers. Make a display of new words children have learned. Record work as you have planned it. Have a debriefing session with children to reinforce what they have learned.

School visits are exhausting but worth while. Things do not just happen, and success only comes with hard work, careful planning and consultation, and extreme vigilance on the part of all the adults.

OVER TO YOU

1. If you had a longer time to work with children on this topic, what other experiments could you do with an environmental focus? For example, organic gardening, soil erosion, fertiliser run-off, the effects of pollution on plants in the locality...

2. The other year-groups in the school were focusing on cooking and the social aspects of food, packaging and advertising, cooking and physical processes, world food distribution and famine, and diet and health. What environmental or sustainability issues would be relevant in these cases?

3. Using the section on planning a farm visit as a basis, write yourself an action plan for a visit to somewhere else, for example: a train station, a supermarket, a museum of local history...

RESOURCES

Curriculum Materials

FOOD, FARMS AND FUTURES: THE ORGANIC OPTION

Primary Pack, Soil Association. See address below, price £5.00.

An excellent pack, from which some of the activities in this topic plan are taken. There are ten information sheets and ten sheets of suggestions for activities.

DATA HANDLING IN PRIMARY SCIENCE

National Council for Educational Technology.

This is a computer software package. As a student, you will not be in a position to buy it, but it is worth asking if your school has this or something similar.

If you are planning a topic on other food issues, such as world distribution, trade, famine, etc. both the following organisations have a great deal of suitable material:

Oxfam Education, 274 Banbury Road, Oxford OX2 7DZ

Christian Aid, 35 Lower Marsh, London SE1 7TL

NON-FICTION

CHILDREN NEED FOOD

Harry Undy, Save the Children/Wayland, 1987.

This has a useful chapter on food production, well illustrated with photographs. Other sections include the pleasure of food and food sharing. There is a useful address list.

FOOD FOR THOUGHT, GILL STANDRING

A & C Black, 1990.

A good starting point for discussion on the issues of agribusiness and organic farming. It also has useful sections on other food issues such as processed and packaged food, fresh and local produce.

FOOD PLANTS

Jennifer Cochrane, Heinemann, 1990.

A wide-ranging book covering types of food plants, crop husbandry, monoculture and chemical inputs, as well as other food issues such as food mountains, famine and food plants for the future. Suitable for top of the age-range or more able children.

MUCK AND MAGIC

Jo Readman, Heinemann Library, 1993.

An excellent, well illustrated book for children, explaining the principles of organic gardening. There are basic scientific explanations, simple experiments and advice on growing a number of different plants without the use of chemicals.

PESTICIDES AND FERTILISERS IN FARMING

Ron Taylor, Watts, 1990.

A book for more able children introducing the issues and contrasting 'artificial' and 'natural' farming.

WASTE NOT, WANT NOT: FOOD

Anne-Marie Constant, Burke Books, 1984.

Easy reading, with the concepts well illustrated. It has sections on food chains and pesticide concentrations, as well as covering other food issues such as desertification and how food is shared between rich and poor.

Fiction, Fiction Books and Reference Books

ADDRESSES

THE HENRY DOUBLEDAY RESEARCH ASSOCIATION

The National Centre for Organic Gardening, Ryton-on-Dunsmore, Coventry CV8 3LG. Tel: 01203 303517.
Researches, demonstrates and promotes environmentally friendly growing techniques. They have information leaflets and other publications and will willingly give advice.

NATIONAL FARMERS' UNION

Head Office, 22 Long Acre, London WC2E 9LY.
They will give you the address of your regional office, who will in turn give you a list of farms, including organic, who will take a school visit.

PARENTS FOR SAFE FOOD

Britannia House, 1–11 Glenthorpe Road, London W6 OLF.
Aims to increase public awareness of some of the potential health hazards in our foods, and campaigns to make food safer. Supplies information leaflets (adult level) on specific topics.

SOIL ASSOCIATION

Organic Food and Farming Centre, 86–88 Colston Street, Bristol BS1 5BB.
Promotes organic farming and acts as a consumer watchdog on food quality issues. They have an extensive book catalogue and are currently increasing their range of educational materials. Will supply a list of organic farms which can be visited. Members receive the journal, *Living Earth*.

If you are interested in including husbandry in your topic, it might be worth contacting the following:

COMPASSION IN WORLD FARMING TRUST

Charles House, 5A Charles Street, Petersfield, Hampshire GU32 3EH. Telephone: 01730 268070.

ROYAL SOCIETY FOR THE PREVENTION OF CRUELTY TO ANIMALS

Causeway, Horsham, West Sussex RH12 1HG.

THE VEGETARIAN SOCIETY

Parkdale, Dunham Road, Altrincham, Cheshire WA14 4QG.

FOOD AND FARMING INFORMATION SERVICE

National Agricultural Centre, Stoneleigh, Warwickshire CV8 2LZ. Telephone: 01203 696969.

WHERE NEXT?

When you finish your training and have your magic piece of paper stating that you are, at last, qualified to teach, you will probably heave a great sigh of relief. But this, of course, is not the end of your learning. Continuous professional development is the key to good teaching and to personal satisfaction – not to say, promotion.

When you take up your first post, the amount of support you get will depend on the school and the policies of the local education authority. You will be able to learn a great deal from colleagues, not just by observing what they do but by asking questions, requesting advice, discussing problems... Don't be afraid of this – they were all new teachers once. Don't forget, though, that they may also want to learn from you. Coming straight from your recent training, you may be able to offer fresh ideas and certainly fresh enthusiasms. We hope one of your enthusiasms will be for Environmental Education.

You will (of course) keep up with your reading of professional books and journals. There are many books on environmental issues and Environmental Education; and more are being published all the time. Some of these will give you quite different perspectives from those offered in this book. You can also learn a great deal by reading the handbooks which accompany teaching packs and schemes. Throughout your career there will be opportunities to go on short or long-term courses and you can make sure you get the maximum benefit from working with any advisory teachers visiting your school. But the best form of professional development is that which you do for yourself, and this applies as much to Environmental Education as to any other area of the curriculum.

Just as we advocate 'active learning' for children, the best way to continue your own education is to be directly involved in it. Ian Robottom (1987) says that teachers' professional development should be enquiry based, participatory and practice based, critical, community based and collaborative. This is remarkably similar to Christiane Dorion's list of teaching strategies appropriate for Environmental Education in the classroom, quoted on page 43. To expand slightly: 'enquiry based' in this context means that teachers should research in a systematic and scientific way into their own practice; 'participatory and practice based' means the teacher is involved in addressing her or his own problems; being 'critical' implies a critique of current environmental and educational practices and developing one's own theories; by 'community-based' Robottom means that a teacher's professional development in environmental

education should be firmly based on local environmental issues (although 'local' can mean the whole country) and local classroom conditions; and finally, he suggests that 'collaborative' development is necessary, not only because 'several heads are better than one', but because if measures need to be taken which involve challenging authority or institutions, collective action is likely to be more effective than individual.

A term much used in professional development circles these days is 'action research'. It can be used for improving your own practice (How can I adapt this learning task to suit all abilities?); for curriculum planning (Which topic is best suited to help children understand extinction?); or for solving a particular problem in the classroom (Why do my class find it so hard to collaborate?).

There are many definitions of action research but at its simplest level it is the familiar 'plan, teach, review' cycle which most teachers employ all the time. But it should mean more than this. It is a more systematic and conscious process. Here is our version:

1 First, identify the issue. Be as precise as you can. Break it down into steps if necessary and perhaps tackle one step at a time. Work with colleagues wherever appropriate.

2 Plan what you are going to do about it, drawing on previous experience, advice from colleagues, theoretical knowledge, logic and/or intuition. Also plan how you intend to monitor what happens. Maybe you will fill in a daily diary, maybe you will give the children a questionnaire or tick boxes in a matrix...

3 Put your plan into action and make sure you consciously observe and record its course.

4 Analyse your findings and reflect on them, again with colleagues if possible. Did you achieve the desired result? Did it work for some children and not others? Have there been any noticeable behaviour changes? What was the most/least successful element? Have you changed any of your initial assumptions? Is it the school system itself which hindered the progress? Is the suggested National Curriculum level inappropriate here?

5 ...which may well lead to making a new plan.

THE TRADITIONAL SPIRAL OF ACTION RESEARCH CYCLES

One cycle of PLANNING, ACTING, OBSERVING, REFLECTING is usually followed by several more before the problem is really solved to everyone's satisfaction (see diagram). As the problem recedes and your teaching improves, you should have a clearer grasp of the ideas or theory which can best inform your practice, and the social structures and relations which best facilitate the kinds of education you wish to promote in your school and community. You can take greater control over your working life as a teacher and are more likely to be able to educate for sustainability.

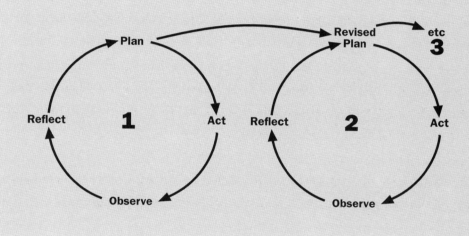

This process of continuous evaluation and reflection is not confined to Environmental Education, of course. As a practising teacher you will have many day-to-day and long-term concerns – the detailed requirements of the National Curriculum, problems of individual children, pressure from governors and parents, impending visits from inspectors! However, action research is particularly appropriate to Environmental Education as they share the premise that people should take responsibility for changes which affect them.

It would be worth while keeping to hand some kind of statement which sums up your views on Environmental Education. It could be the 'nine principles for a sustainable society' from Caring for the Earth (see page 25); it could be one of the quotations in Parts 4 or 5 of this book or the school's own policy statement; or it might be a set of aims you have written yourself. Refer to it occasionally and ask yourself what you have done recently to further those aims and what you could do tomorrow/next week/ next term...

LOOKING INWARDS

As well as using action research to explore what you do, it is important that you should sometimes turn the spotlight inwards to examine what you think. This may happen, of course, in the course of an action research as outlined above – you might find that the answer to a problem is a change in your own behaviour or ideas. But you could also make a conscious effort sometimes to reflect on your beliefs. Where have they come from? Are they really your own? Do they still hold in the light of changes in society/the environmental crisis/movements in education? Have you really considered alternative views put by colleagues or in something you have read? There are lots of people out there writing books and articles about pedagogical theory, society, environment, development, global education... This is not to say that you should slavishly follow any new trend, but you do need to keep an open mind. One of the precepts which is always emphasised in education nowadays is that we must educate children for change, because the world is changing at an ever-increasing rate. If it is important for children, it must be just as important for us as educators.

"Honest hope derives from a belief that positive change is possible in the world. And we will only achieve this if we experience ourselves changing. The key is risk, doing that which we thought we could not do.

FRANCES MOORE LAPPE

A certain amount of private navel-gazing can be useful, but it is sometimes more constructive to work with colleagues. In the early days at your school, you probably won't be in a position to have a great deal of influence, but once you are on surer ground, you could suggest – if it does not already happen – that some staff meetings or training sessions are given over to a critique of current ideas, beliefs, the school ethos... Education ministers come and go, the National Curriculum mutates, the local authority changes political colour, but the school goes on. Every teacher needs to be clear where they stand and why they stand there.

YOU AND YOUR CLASSROOM

If you have got this far in the book, you have already read most of what we have to say about classroom practice, but once you have your own class, you will have more scope than you have on teaching practice. You will, of course, need to follow the National Curriculum and the plans and guidelines the school has drawn up, but it is the teacher who has the task of creating content and coherence and setting the tone of the classroom. If you wish your children to 'care for their own environment' and 'contribute to decisions that affect them' (*Caring for the Earth*) you could, for example, involve them in planning the layout of the classroom.

Even if the school is not environmentally oriented, you can take small steps with your class – they could be the spearhead to a new awareness! They could carry out audits of their classroom waste or energy use. Perhaps they might take responsibility for one of the public areas of the school and undertake to keep it attractive and welcoming; you could discuss with the rest of the staff the possibility of your class painting murals on the wall outside your classroom or of planting butterfly attractive plants outside your windows...

When you get to know the neighbourhood of your school, you will have opportunities to investigate local issues with the children, something that may not have been possible on teaching practice. It might be ongoing problems, such as difficulties children have in crossing a busy road, dog fouling of the streets, lack of recycling facilities in the area; or it might be a current controversy, such as council plans to redevelop waste land or a decision to axe a local bus route.

YOU AND YOUR SCHOOL

As you gain more experience you will be involved more and more in general school planning. In a good school the whole staff will be engaged in curriculum development and there will also be periodic evaluation of practices and values. The school needs systematic planning to take account of National Curriculum Subject Orders, cross-curricular themes, dimensions and skills, the school's place in the community, the wishes of parents, governors and the local authority, and, above all, what it wants for its children.

"The whole curriculum of a school, of course, goes far beyond the formal timetable. It involves a range of policies and practices to promote the personal and social development of pupils...

To achieve these whole curriculum aims, schools need to ensure that the planned contribution of different subjects is not made in isolation but in the light of their contribution to pupils' learning as a whole...

Cross-curricular themes have been identified to achieve these whole curriculum aims. These are elements that enrich the educational experience of pupils..."

NATIONAL CURRICULUM COUNCIL CIRCULAR 6

"*Education for sustainability is a state of awareness which builds on current good practice and should be part of everything we teach, in much the way that our teaching of equal opportunities has become.*"

GILLIAN SYMONS,
REACHING OUT

If a school can keep this in mind, there is less chance that Environmental Education – one of the 'cross-curricular themes' – will be seen as a bolt-on extra. It may be your role to ensure that it is not marginalised. Of course, you cannot expect to bring about instant change, but once you are feeling confident, you could begin to put out feelers. There are a number of publications from WWF which are aimed at whole-school development in Environmental Education. They are listed in the Resources Section. Of course what you do in your own classroom is vital, but to achieve real results, the whole school community should share common aims.

"*Environmental Education deals with values. Many school systems regard this as dangerous ground, and many teachers … are not trained to teach values. The 'whole school' approach, in which the school tries to behave consistently with what is taught, may also be dauntingly novel. Yet no lifestyle or education system is value-free. It is vital that schools teach the right skills for sustainable living. It is equally important that what the school does reinforces what it teaches.*"

CARING FOR THE EARTH, PAGE 55

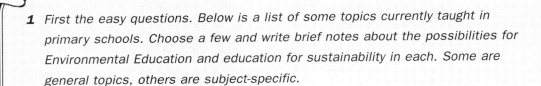

OVER TO YOU

1 *First the easy questions. Below is a list of some topics currently taught in primary schools. Choose a few and write brief notes about the possibilities for Environmental Education and education for sustainability in each. Some are general topics, others are subject-specific.*

Invaders and settlers, The school neighbourhood, Our pets, A village in India, Our school, Weather, Electricity, People who help us, Change, Victorian Britain, Keeping healthy, Migration, The supermarket...

2 *This time the list of topics are in themselves more or less 'environmental'. What specific subject areas of the National Curriculum could they serve?*

Energy, Forests, Waste, Planet Earth, The sea, Endangered species, Pollution, Minibeasts...

3 And now the harder questions. Suppose you take up your first appointment in a school where Environmental Education is given very low priority. In fact, it occurs only where is it is specifically part of the National Curriculum Subject Orders. The headteacher knows from your application and interview that you are interested in this area and invites you to address a staff meeting. Make detailed notes about what you would say to convince your colleagues that Environmental Education (and education for sustainability, if you feel brave enough) should be an integral part of the school curriculum. Bear in mind possible arguments that other staff members might have ready for you ("the timetable is already too crowded... Too controversial... We already do it in Geography and Science...") What evidence would you quote? Are there strategies you could use apart from a straight talk?

4 The staff and head are duly convinced. They ask you to write a policy statement on Environmental Education which can be included in the school's prospectus. You, of course, point out that such a statement should be the result of staff debate and negotiation, but nevertheless you go away and write your own version for later discussion. Remember the audience. A school prospectus is for parents, prospective parents, governors, members of the local community, new teachers and inspectors, as well as being a reminder for the current staff about what the school policies are. It should be brief, to the point and jargon-free as far as possible; it should outline both what the school believes and how it intends to put the theory into practice.

5 As we have seen, one of the aims of Environmental Education is to change people's attitudes. Have any of your attitudes changed through reading this book and working on the tasks?

REFERENCES
I Robottom, **"TOWARDS INQUIRY-BASED PROFESSIONAL DEVELOPMENT IN ENVIRONMENTAL EDUCATION"** *in I Robottom (ed)* **ENVIRONMENTAL EDUCATION: PRACTICE AND POSSIBILITY**, *Deakin University Press, 1987*

Resources

GREENING THE STAFFROOM

G Pike and D Selby, WWF-UK/The Centre for Global Education/BBC Education, 1990

An excellent compendium of ideas for staff development in Environmental Education, including suggestions for running in-service courses. The activities emphasise the importance of participatory and co-operative learning.

GREENPRINTS FOR CHANGING SCHOOLS

S Greig, G Pike, D Selby, WWF-UK/The Centre for Global Education/Kogan Page, 1989

A thought-provoking book which links the theory and practice of educational change. It shows how successful educational change in the school depends on changes at the personal level.

EDUCATION FOR SUSTAINABILITY

John Huckle and Stephen Stirling (eds), WWF-UK/Earthscan, 1996.

This brings together contributions from environmental educators working at all levels and provides perspectives on the philosophy, politics and pedagogy of education for sustainability, as well as case studies and guides toward good practice.

THE HANDBOOK OF ENVIRONMENTAL EDUCATION

Joy Palmer and Philip Neal, Routledge, 1994.

An excellent and comprehensive guide containing advice on policy, staff motivation, planning and assessment, as well as extensive lists for further information.

LET'S REACH OUT (PRIMARY)

Gillian Symons and Ken Webster, WWF-UK, 1994

This handbook is designed for teachers who have responsibility for cross-curricular themes, particularly Environmental Education. It contains a rationale for education for sustainability, briefings for colleagues and ideas for INSET.

PLANNING AND EVALUATION OF ENVIRONMENTAL EDUCATION IN PRIMARY SCHOOLS

C Dorion, WWF-UK/CEE/The University of Reading, 1993

This is a very useful pack for anyone who wants to evaluate their own classroom practices, or for those responsible for Environmental Education in their school. The material is based on the work of teachers and advisers.

OUR WORLD – OUR RESPONSIBILITY ENVIRONMENTAL EDUCATION – A PRACTICAL GUIDE. *RSPC/CEE, 1996.*

This gives practical advice on developing and implementing environmental education policies in schools. It includes case studies and sources of further information.

THE SCHOOL IS US: A PRACTICAL GUIDE TO SUCCESSFUL WHOLE SCHOOL CHANGE

Linnea Renton, WWF-UK/Manchester Development Education Project, 1993

The subtitle says it all. The activities emphasise collective responsibility for the school's future, whether in setting targets, identifying blocks, developing better communications and decision-making procedures or improving staff meetings.

HOW TO FIND OUT MORE

Curriculum materials

Two major sources of information and classroom materials on relevant issues are WWF-UK (World Wide Fund For Nature) and Oxfam. They include books for teachers, games, activity packs, information sheets. Schools should have their catalogues, but if not you could send for one. Further information and addresses below. Some of the WWF publications relevant for primary teachers are listed below.

Another very useful address when looking for resources is: **Council for Environmental Education,** University of Reading, London Road, Reading RG1 5AQ. Tel: 01734 756061 CEE co-ordinates and promotes environmental education in England, Wales and Northern Ireland. They produce a range of publications including a series of printed information sheets, resource lists and in-service training materials. Please send an SAE for publications and price list.

ACTIVE MATHS

Margaret Williams, Toni Macpherson, Margaret Mackintosh, Michael Williams, WWF-UK, 1991
A handbook for teachers at Key Stage 1, placing emphasis on enjoyment and appreciation of the environment as first steps towards an active concern for the future.

CATCHING THE LIGHT

Brian Moses, WWF-UK, 1991
A book of practical suggestions for classroom activities and discussions for 5–8 year olds, linking language and environment. They are nearly all based on the child's own familiar surroundings. There are poems and prose written by both children and adults.

CURRICULUM GUIDANCE 3: THE WHOLE CURRICULUM, *NCC, 1990*
CURRICULUM GUIDANCE 7: ENVIRONMENTAL EDUCATION, *NCC, 1990*

These are the National Curriculum documents (England and Wales) most relevant here (unless they have been updated by the time you read this). There should be copies in every school, but if you would like your own they can be obtained from SCAA, Newcombe House, 45 Notting Hill Gate, London W11 3JB.

ENVIRONMENTAL EDUCATION: A FRAMEWORK FOR THE DEVELOPMENT OF A CROSS-CURRICULAR THEME IN WALES, ADVISORY PAPER 17

Curriculum Council for Wales, 1992
The Welsh equivalent of *Curriculum Guidance 7,* above.

NATIONAL GUIDELINES: ENVIRONMENTAL STUDIES 5–14

The Scottish Office, 1993

LEARNING FOR LIFE: A NATIONAL STRATEGY FOR ENVIRONMENTAL EDUCATION IN SCOTLAND

The Scottish Office, 1993

EARTHRIGHTS: EDUCATION AS IF THE PLANET REALLY MATTERED

Sue Greig, Graham Pike and David Selby WWF-UK/ The Centre for Global Education/Kogan Page, 1987, reprinted 1990 . ISBN 1 85091 453 2 (Kogan Page) ISBN 1 947613 02 1 (WWF)
A compendium of ideas, facts, quotations, reports, discussions, school case studies and activities. It makes links with human rights, peace and development studies and stresses that the school itself and its ways of working should reflect the ideals, encouraging personal growth and self esteem.

PART 11

Curriculum materials (cont'd)

GLOBAL PERSPECTIVES IN THE NATIONAL CURRICULUM: GUIDANCE FOR KEY STAGES 1 AND 2.

Cathy Midwinter (ed), DEA, 1995.

The title says it all; this is a slim but invaluable book which shows how children's global awareness can be developed as part of everyday classroom activities.

THE GREEN UMBRELLA

Jill Brand, A & C Black/WWF-UK, 1991

This is a collection of material on 'green' themes for use in school assemblies. Although it is unlikely you will be called on to take an assembly just yet, you might find some of the poetry, prose, facts and discussion points useful in the classroom. Many schools have this book lurking in a cupboard so it is worth asking.

HOW TO GREEN YOUR SCHOOL (PRIMARY)

Friends of the Earth (address below)

Combines learning with environmental action. A series of surveys highlighting the practical links between understanding the issues and what people can do about them. Action sheets and teacher's notes.

IT'S OUR WORLD TOO

Birmingham Development Education Centre/South Yorkshire Development Education Centre, 1992. Available from Birmingham DEC, Gillett Centre, 998 Bristol Road, Selly Oak, Birmingham B29 6LE. Also available from Oxfam. £8.40

A handbook for teachers about the relationship between local environmental issues and those facing people in other parts of the world. Full of practical suggestions for exploring the issues with children.

LEARNING FROM EXPERIENCE: WORLD STUDIES IN THE PRIMARY CURRICULUM

Miriam Steiner, Trentham Books, 1993

Not strictly environmental education, but an excellent source of advice and suggestions for bringing a global perspective and experiential activities to the everyday curriculum.

MY WORLD

WWF-UK/Scholastic, 1992

A resource pack of nine themed booklets and an introductory guide to help teachers of primary children deliver the science curriculum with an environmental focus.

PEOPLE AND THEIR COMMUNITIES

Prue Poulton and Gillian Symons, WWF-UK, 1993

A practical teaching resource designed to help children at Key Stages 2/3 understand their own place in the community and how communities work. There are activities for children and teachers' notes.

SOMEWHERE TO BE

Brian Moses, WWF-UK, 1992

A companion volume to *Catching the Light* (see above) but aimed at teachers of 9–12 year-olds, with content matter covering wider environmental issues.

TEACHING ENVIRONMENTAL MATTERS THROUGH THE NATIONAL CURRICULUM

SCAA, 1996

This booklet, commissioned by the Secretary of State for Education and Employment, sets out guidance on teaching and planning at all key stages and through all subjects, illustrated with case studies of good practice.

WINDOWS TO NATURE

Mildred Masheder, WWF-UK

This book gives teachers of nursery and infants children ideas for encouraging them to learn about and enjoy the wonders of the natural world. The activity-based approach provides opportunities for much 'hands-on' experimentation and exploration.

BRIGHT SPARKS

An Introduction to Environmental Education for Primary Trainee Teachers

By Jill Brand and Clare Marlow

© **WWF-UK (World Wide Fund For Nature), 1997**

All rights reserved. The material in this publication may be photocopied
for use within the purchasing school only. No reproduction, copy or
transmission of this publication may otherwise be made without the prior
written permission of the publisher.

Published by WWF-UK (World Wide Fund For Nature),
Panda House, Weyside Park, Godalming, Surrey GU7 1XR, UK.

A catalogue record for this book is available from The British Library.

ISBN: 0 947613 75 7

This book is printed on recycled paper.

Designed by: Quadraphic Design, West Byfleet, Surrey.
Printed by: Optichrome Limited, Woking, Surrey.

WWF-UK is a Registered Charity No. 201707

Acknowledgement

Cartoons © 1971 by Norman Thelwell. Reproduced from
"The Effluent Society", first published 1971 by Methuen Co. Ltd.
Magnum edition published 1978.
Reproduced by permission of Reed Consumer Books Ltd.

Information books for adults

GENERAL READING

BLUEPRINT FOR A GREEN PLANET

John Seymour and Herbert Girardet, Dorling Kindersley, 1987 ISBN 0 86318 178 3

One of the best of the many books on the market which both sets out the problems and suggests how we as individuals can help to solve them by changing our behaviour and by more careful shopping.

EARTHRISE

Herbert Girardet, Paladin, 1992

This gives an overview of the mess our world is in. It is written for the layperson by someone who is both knowledgeable and passionate. Its central message is that we must change our attitudes, not tinker at the edges with technological fixes.

THE EARTH REPORT 3

Edward Goldsmith and Nicholas Hildyard (eds), Mitchell Beazley, 1992

This is out of print, but you may be still able to find a copy.An alphabetically arranged encyclopaedia of all the current issues. For hard-hitting facts, this is a must.

OUR COMMON FUTURE: A READER'S GUIDE

Don Hinrichsen, IIED/Earthscan 1986, reprinted 1989

This is the 'Bruntland Report' on Environment and Development. It presents the stark facts about how environmental degradation and unfair trading between rich and poor affects the lives of people throughout the world, and the Commission's recommendations are also given.

JOURNALS

THE ENVIRONMENT DIGEST

Environmental Publications Ltd, Panther House, 38 Mount Pleasant, London WC1X OAP

A monthly digest of environment and conservation news, culled largely from newspapers and weekly journals, with some information from the specialist press.

THE ECOLOGIST

Subscriptions c/o RED Computing, The Outback, 58–60 Kingston Road, New Malden, Surrey KT3 3LZ

Six issues a year, each containing a number of in-depth articles on environment and development plus short reports. There is also news on current campaigns and suggestions for appropriate action.

NEW INTERNATIONALIST

PO Box 79, Hertford SG14 1AQ.

A monthly journal, each with a main theme, covering issues of poverty, inequality, rights, environment, power etc. Thought provoking and full of useful facts and figures.

Books for children

There are now very many books for children about environmental issues, both those giving general information and advice about what we can do and those giving information on specific subjects, such as rainforests or energy. Most educational publishers have series of the latter kind and school libraries should have a good selection. It is especially worth while looking out for Wayland books, which seem to be particularly well thought out and presented. The more general books are mainly for the home market, but you may find it useful to invest in one or two or borrow them from the local library. The information may be in a more usable form than in those for adults. Here are just a few:

GOING GREEN AT HOME AND SCHOOL

Wayland/FoE 1993

One of the best books for children about what we can do to help solve the problems, particularly at a local level. Well written and illustrated and, unusually, printed on recycled paper.

IAN AND FRED'S BIG GREEN BOOK

Fred Pearce, ill. Ian Winton, Kingfisher Books, 1991

This is a book for top juniors or secondary school pupils, but it has some delightful illustrations which any junior children could enjoy and learn from – the city as an all-devouring machine-monster, for example, or trees with roots like hands holding the soil in place. It explains simply how, left to itself, the Earth and the things that live on it maintain a healthy balance of gases, water, temperature and so on, and how humans are interfering too much.

MY FIRST GREEN BOOK

Angela Wilkes, Dorling Kindersley, 1991,
ISBN 0 86318 623 8

A large format, glossy book with uncluttered photographs – some life-size – and straightforward information in short clear chunks. There are easy-to-follow instructions for a few experiments and activities. A good introduction to some issues (but a bit over-the-top on presentation?).

RESCUE MISSION PLANET EARTH: A CHILDREN'S EDITION OF AGENDA 21

Kingfisher Books/Peace Child International in asssociation with the United Nations, 1994

The best description of this book is taken from its its back cover: "Thousands of kids from nearly 100 countries have worked together in an extraordinary effort to find out what exactly was in [*Agenda 21*]. This unique book is designed, written and illustrated by children for children to inspire young people all over the world to join the rescue mission to save our planet, our only home." While you wouldn't give it to a junior child to read in its entirety, there are poems, pictures and individual pieces of writing it would be well worth sharing.

THE YOUNG GREEN CONSUMER GUIDE

John Elkington and Julia Hailes, Victor Gollancz 1990
ISBN 0 575 04722 4

There are four sections in this book: the first presents the global issues; the second shows how what we do at home affects them; the third is about school and the last gives lots of ideas for positive action children can take. It is well presented and illustrated with colour cartoons throughout. Suitable for older children, but useful information and ideas you could mediate for younger ones.

Information can also be obtained from some of the organisations opposite.

Organisations

COUNCIL FOR ENVIRONMENTAL EDUCATION

School of Education, University of Reading, London Road, Reading RG1 5AQ Tel: 01734 756061

CEE co-ordinates and promotes Environmental Education in England, Wales and Northern Ireland. They produce a range of publications including a series of printed information sheets and in-service training materials. Please send an SAE for publications and price list.

DEVELOPMENT EDUCATION ASSOCIATION

29–31 Cowper Street, London EC2A 4AP. Tel: 0171 490 8108.

The DEA is a national umbrella organisation which supports and promotes the work of all those engaged in bringing about a better public understanding of global and development issues. They have an increasing number of useful publications.

FRIENDS OF THE EARTH

26–28 Underwood Street, London N1 7JQ

One of the major national campaigning organisations with groups which also work on local issues. Members receive a quarterly journal full of current news. They have a wide range of publications, including information sheets for children. By joining a scheme called 'School Friends' teachers can receive the journal, packs of educational material and a discount on other FoE publications.

INTERNATIONAL CENTRE FOR CONSERVATION EDUCATION

Greenfield House, Guiting Power, Cheltenham, Gloucestershire GL54 5TZ

ICCE markets a large selection of audiovisual material, much of which is suitable for primary children. Send for list.

OXFAM

272 Banbury Road, Oxford OX2 7DZ. Tel: 01865 56777

As well as raising money for urgent relief programmes and long term development, Oxfam promotes public awareness of the links between environmental degradation and world poverty. They have an extensive education catalogue.

SCOTTISH ENVIRONMENTAL EDUCATION COUNCIL (SEEC)

Department of Environmental Science, University of Stirling, Stirling FK9 4LA. Tel: 01786 467867.

A very useful first point of contact through which schools can reach a wide range of organisations offering support for Environmental Education.

WOMEN'S ENVIRONMENTAL NETWORK TRUST (WEN)

Aberdeen Studios, 22 Highbury Grove, London N5 2EA. Tel: 0171 354 8823

A source of information on a range of environmental issues; they produce a Newsletter, publications list and provide a consumer advice line, WENDi (Women's Environmental Network Directory of Information). Please send an A4 SAE with a 29p stamp for an information pack.

WWF-UK (WORLD WIDE FUND FOR NATURE)

Panda House, Weyside Park, Godalming, Surrey GU7 1XR. Tel: 01483 426444

See 'About WWF' on page iii.

YOUNG PEOPLE'S TRUST FOR THE ENVIRONMENT AND NATURE CONSERVATION

8 Leapdale Road, Guildford, Surrey GU1 4JX

The trust encourages active participation by young people. They run courses, holidays, and expeditions, publish fact sheets and a newsletter and will answer all kinds of queries if a stamped addressed envelope is sent.

INSET

Local Education Authorities, Universities and other independent organisations run in-service courses, some of which address Environmental Education, Development Education and other related themes. Look out for these from the INSET co-ordinator in your school, or from your LEA contact. In particular, WWF-UK runs short courses on education for sustainability, details of which can be obtained from their Teacher Education section at the address listed above.